7 Simple Steps
to Green Your Church

Also available

Green Church:
Reduce, Reuse,
Recycle, Rejoice!
Book

Green Church:
Reduce, Reuse,
Recycle, Rejoice!
Leader Guide

Burst:
Green Church
A Study for Youth

Green Church:
Caretakers of
God's Creation
A Study for Children

7 Simple Steps to Green Your Church

Rebekah Simon-Peter

Abingdon Press
Nashville

7 SIMPLE STEPS
TO GREEN YOUR CHURCH
by Rebekah Simon-Peter

Copyright © 2010 by Abingdon Press

Scripture quotations in this publication, unless otherwise indicated, are from the New Revised Standard Version of the Bible, copyrighted © 1989 by the Division of Christian Education of the National Council of the Churches of Christ in the United States of America, and are used by permission.

This book is printed on recycled paper.

Library of Congress Cataloging-in-Publication Data

Simon-Peter, Rebekah.
  7 simple steps to green your church / Rebekah Simon-Peter.
    p. cm.
  Includes bibliographical references.
  ISBN 978-1-4267-0293-8 (binding: book - pbk./trade pbk., adhesive, perfect binding : alk. paper) 1. Environmentalism—United States—Popular works. 2. Sustainable living—United States—Popular works. 3. Human ecology—United States—Popular works. 4. Nature—Effect of human beings on—United States—Popular works. I. Title. II. Title: Seven simple steps to green your church.
  GE197.S56 2010
  261.8′8—dc22

2010002101

FSC
Mixed Sources
Product group from well-managed forests, controlled sources and recycled wood or fiber
Cert no. SCS-COC-002464
www.fsc.org
©1996 Forest Stewardship Council

10 11 12 13 14 15 16 17 18 19—10 9 8 7 6 5 4 3 2 1

Manufactured in the United States of America

To future generations, with love and hope

Contents

Introduction

He has told you, O mortal, what is good;
and what does the LORD require of you
but to do justice, and to love kindness,
and to walk humbly with your God?
Micah 6:8

This is a book about greening your church over the course of one year—step by step, task by task, ministry by ministry. It is not about theory or theology; for that, consider using the companion book, *Green Church: Reduce, Reuse, Recycle, Rejoice!* which gives biblical and scientific support to the vital task of caring for creation and which is designed for individual and group study.

The yearlong process of greening your church will join you to people around the country and around the world, groups of dedicated and inspiring people who are living as if the rest of creation mattered. Catalysts in their communities of faith, they are greening their congregations and reclaiming the word *stewardship.*

Living as if Creation Mattered

You will meet many dedicated people in the pages of this book, such as 26-year-old United Methodist associate minister Jordan Thrasher from Chamblee, Georgia, who is redefining progress for his community; Mother Shepherd, the first female rector in her historically African American Episcopal congregation, who is finding a way to institutionalize environmental stewardship; Anglican Karen Chalk, the chemist- turned-priest who has led her Canadian congregation in installing energy-efficient heating and cooling while raising summer worship attendance; and Travis Dollar, whose Eagle Scout project enabled a whole city to recycle.

These people are not alone. They are representative of a growing movement that includes theological liberals and conservatives, mainline and non-denominational, and spans every branch of Christendom—Orthodox, Catholic, and Protestant.[1] Across the religious spectrum Jews, Muslims, Hindus, Buddhists, and others are also heeding their sacred teachings and going green. At last, our consciousness as persons of faith is shifting, aligning us with native and indigenous peoples who have kept these truths alive for centuries.

We hope that it is not too late.

The Power of the Faith Community

The US Environmental Protection Agency has estimated that if America's more than 300,000 houses of worship cut back energy use by a mere ten percent, we could save nearly $200 million for missions. We could make available more than 5.4 billion kilowatt hours of electricity without additional cost or pollution. We could also prevent the emission of more than two million tons of greenhouse gases. That is an amount equivalent to taking 400,000 cars off the road or planting over a half million acres of trees.[2]

For most churches, a ten percent reduction in energy use is easily within reach, as are significant savings on energy costs. Other churches can manage far more than that.

This book will show you how.

How the Book Is Organized

This volume is divided into two parts. Part One, "7 Simple Steps," contains a step-by-step approach to greening your church over the course of one year, with a list of tasks for each step. Following these steps will help ensure that creation care becomes deeply incorporated into the life of your church. Worksheets are provided at the website, *greenchurch.cokesbury.com.*

Part Two, "Areas of Focus," lays out twelve areas of church life to be addressed, one per month over the course of a year, from worship to missions to the grounds. In each area, three levels of commitment are offered: "The Basics," "Get Creative," and "Go All Out." Choose how green you want to go. Success stories round out each area, showing what other churches have accomplished.

An appendix, "Building Green," offers insight into green construction from the ground up. The website, *greenchurch.cokesbury.com*, has been designed to complement *Green Church: Reduce, Reuse, Recyle, Rejoice!* and 7 SIMPLE STEPS TO GREEN YOUR CHURCH. Go there to download worksheets, get more resources, find helpful links, and stay inspired. You are part of the worldwide movement that loves God, respects the earth, and recognizes our interdependence with the rest of creation. Stay connected to it!

How to Use This Book

Designed with flexibility in mind, this book can be used in a variety of ways. It can be a stand-alone handbook or part of a Green Church study. One person might catch the vision and share this book with others; or it can serve as a hands-on guide for small groups, Sunday school classes, and church boards. Remember to include the youth and children in the activities.

In fact, I urge you to include the whole congregation in the task of going green, at church and at home. The care of creation concerns all who live on Planet Earth. The more we participate in greening our lives, the more empowered we will be. As you switch to compact fluorescent light bulbs (CFLs) at church, ask people to do so at home. As you repair leaks and you weather-strip doors and windows in your buildings, invite members to do the same at home.

Remember to ask members to keep track of the changes they make at home so that at year's end you can report total savings and changes. Include these numbers in your celebration service.

Get the Big Picture

To get started, skim the whole book so as to keep the big picture in mind. In Part One, note how to form a Green Team, and consider the people you would like to include (Step 1). Begin to think about calculating your church's carbon footprint (Step 2). Sketch out a few of the actions you will want to include in your plan (Step 3). Generate excitement with your team about taking action (Step 4).

Be aware of the need for regular communications along the way (Step 5). Keep in mind the kind of celebration you would like to have at the end (Step 6). Consider who you will want to share your success with when you pay it forward (Step 7).

In Part Two, think about an approach for tackling the twelve areas of focus, one per month, during the coming year. Consider the areas of church life you will focus on and how you will be doing it. Read some of the stewardship success stories in "We Did It!" While no two churches are exactly the same, let the Spirit speak to you about how to adapt the learnings of other churches to your own setting.

Once you have reviewed the big picture, go back to Part One and move prayerfully and deliberately through the seven simple steps. You have a year's worth of tasks and rewards ahead of you.

A Lifelong Journey of Discovery

Keep in mind that greening the church is more than a twelve-month project; it is an ongoing practice. My hope is that as you take these seven simple steps over the next year, you will be drawn into a lifelong journey of discovery about what it means to live sustainably.

As you put your faith into action, know that you are joining a worldwide movement of people who seek to live in peace with all creation and want to pass on a livable world to future generations. May the works of your hands be blessed by God the Creator, Jesus the Redeemer, and the Holy Spirit the Comforter. Amen.

Part One
7 Simple Steps

Step 1. Form a Green Team

"Again, truly I tell you, if two of you agree on earth about anything you ask, it will be done for you by my Father in heaven. For where two or three are gathered in my name, I am there among them."
Matthew 18:19-20

Tasks
- Choose a model
- Recruit team members
- Name the team
- Write a vision statement and goals
- Decide on funding

There is strength in numbers. And there is wisdom. As you begin to green your church, you are going to need help. One person may get the ball rolling, but it helps to have backup. The broader the support you have, the better.

Green teams get formed in many ways: as the result of a Bible study, a common interest such as recycling or gardening, a perceived need for action at your church, a denominational emphasis, or a local environmental crisis. Perhaps your pastor has called you together, or the trustees have decided it is time to save money on utility bills. Maybe you yourself are the green team! You can move forward from any of these starting points.

Choose a Model

Two popular models for church-based green teams seem to work best: the church-wide green team and the small-group green team.

Church-wide Green Team

In the church-wide model, a green team is comprised of key members who have decision-making power, authority, or influence. If possible, include members from some of the following areas:

Clergy/leadership team
Staff
Business manager or church treasurer
Administrative assistant or church secretary
Governing board
Trustees
Christian education department
Women's ministry
Men's ministry
Youth ministry
Missions group
Building manager or custodial services
Groundskeepers
Kitchen staff

Carol Matheis-Kraft says, "At First Congregational United Church of Christ [Longmont, Colorado] we did some things right and some things wrong when we were setting up our zero-waste program. If we were to do it over again, I would suggest a church-wide meeting to make sure we get everyone on board. We had a group of very interested people and Earth Day as a target date; but we didn't have a few key people on board. That would have made a big difference for us."

Small-group Green Team

The second model is the small-group approach. In this model, your green team may be composed of members of a single ministry area such as peace and justice, missions, trustees, or Christian education. Take action where you have the most consensus or authority. Seek the support of your priest or pastor, as well as support from the governing body of your congregation.

As your group grows, try to include people with the knowledge to transform your passion into broader action. Look for the master gardener who understands composting, the engineer who knows the physics of energy, the accountant who can calculate return on investments, the community worker who can organize people to clean up a river, or the blogger who can navigate cyberspace. Do not forget about the extrovert who can throw a good party!

Recruit Team Members

Announcements during worship are a great way to raise awareness about the formation of your green team. Likely, some people will join forces with you this way. Most effective, however, is a personal invitation. People appreciate being asked. Network with key people in the church to find others who may be interested. If your church maintains a talent bank or a spiritual gifts database, use the information to find those who may be professionally employed in a related field.

Holding an initial event is a great way to bring people together. Whether you show an environmentally oriented film, host a lecture, have a potluck, plan a hike, or throw a party, you can attract people through events that combine information with fun. Include people of all ages in your recruiting efforts. Each generation has ideas to contribute and gifts to offer.

Name the Team

Once you gather your group, think of an appropriate name. While Green Team might suit you just fine, consider other possibilities such as Creation Care, Earth Care, Earth Keepers, Ecophilia, Eco-Justice, Eco-Team, Environmental Action, Environmental Stewardship, Go Green, Inconvenient Youth, Sustainability, or Whole Earth.

You can call your group a team, a committee, a task force, a ministry, or an action group. Personally, I prefer *team*. A team plays hard to win at a common goal, while having fun and supporting one another. The game here is working together for the integrity of God's creation. The word *team* also implies action rather than simply meeting or deliberating. Ultimately, the choice is up to you. Choose a name that will energize and motivate you.

Write a Vision Statement and Goals

Now that your group has a name, focus on what you want to do together. A vision statement will help guide you. Consider the aspirations of your team. What do you want to accomplish? For whom? Why?

As you consider these questions, make sure your language is memorable and inspiring. Above all, let it be positive. "Caring for the earth and its resources as God's gifts for sustaining life" will likely get you farther than "Go green or go home!" Remember, however, the shorter the statement, the more likely it is that people will remember it, repeat it, and absorb it.

After you agree on a vision statement, write a list of specific goals that will help bring your vision to life over the next year. When writing the goals, be specific, clear, and concise. Shoot for goals that you can realistically accomplish in one year. "Reduce our carbon footprint 15 percent per year" is do-able and will keep the motivation going. Contrast that with "Use 100 percent renewable energy by 2015." It sounds good, but can you actually accomplish it? If so, go for it. If not, try again.

Once your vision statement and goals are written, use them! Post them on your website. Write and recite them often. Review and refine them as needed.

Decide on Funding

In the long run, going green will save you money. For instance, according to the Energy Star website, "an ENERGY STAR qualified compact fluorescent light bulb (CFL) will save about $30 over its lifetime and pay for itself in about 6 months. It uses 75 percent less energy and lasts about 10 times longer than an incandescent bulb."[3]

In the short term, there will be some costs, so you will need money to work with. If the church budget is tight, you will need to be creative. Not to worry, though. There are a number of ways to fund your greening efforts. Consider the following options.

Special Offerings

Take a collection on Earth Day. Encourage people to make a special donation for a livable planet upon the birth or baptism of a child or a grandchild.

Donations

People love to contribute to a good cause. Do not be afraid to ask for donations. Glen Miles, senior minister at

Country Club Christian Church in Kansas City, Missouri, chuckles as he recalls, "Once our church began to see that we were serious about going green, several people approached me about making donations for our new low-flow toilets. It is not a sexy project, but every bit counts."

Fundraisers

Hold creative fundraisers that advance the goals of going green and fund your next project. Try selling CFLs, garden plants, or worms for compost piles.

BYOM

Ask people to contribute to your green efforts by contributing needed items. Hold a Bring Your Own Mug Sunday to put an end to Styrofoam cup usage. This can also work for cloth napkins, CFLs, seeds for the garden, and a variety of other projects.

Grants and Partnerships

Grants and partnerships may be available to your church through conservation organizations, waste management departments, government entities such as the Environmental Protection Agency and the Department of Energy, and scientific and community organizations. Check with your energy company about rebates for energy-saving projects. Remember to inquire about denominational resources.

Capital Funds

Many churches have monies that can be used only for building improvement and maintenance. By investing those funds in energy-efficient upgrades, your money will do double duty.

Pastor Jeff Rainwater of First United Methodist Church in Laramie, Wyoming, notes, "Using money from our endowment, we bought 40 motion-detector light switches that cost $60-70 each but would save 10 percent in energy use. Even with a 10-year return on investment, it becomes a gift for ministry. That 10 percent savings becomes 10 percent more money that can be used for other things."

Step 2.
Calculate Your Carbon Footprint

*Do you know the balancings of the clouds,
the wondrous works of the one whose
knowledge is perfect?*

Job 37:16

Tasks
- Learn about carbon footprints
- Choose the type of carbon footprint to use
- Collect data
- Input data
- Save your figures

Each of us has an impact on the earth and her natural systems. A carbon footprint is a metaphorical way of describing the depth and width of your impact, especially as it relates to climate change.

When it comes to going green, understanding and calculating your church's carbon footprint is essential. While some churches go green without taking this important step, spending the time to quantify your carbon footprint gives you key baseline information. Once you have this number, you will be able to measure your impact on the climate. Calculating your carbon footprint makes climate change real and going green imperative.

Learn About Carbon Footprints

Carbon Dioxide

Over the last century, the earth's atmosphere has warmed about 1.4 degrees Fahrenheit.[4] While that does not seem like much, it is enough to disrupt the ecological systems upon which life as we know it depends. The polar ice caps are melting, which in turn raises ocean levels. Precipitation patterns are changing, leading to increased flooding and drought. As the soil dries out, there is a greater incidence of forest fires. Warmer air temperatures mean warmer ocean temperatures, which in turn lead to more severe hurricanes and typhoons.

This global warming or climate change, along with pollution and a global population explosion, is wreaking havoc on the creation. It is not just the weather that is changing; songbirds to frogs to polar bears are disappearing. Honeybees and bats are hard hit. With an increase of extreme weather events, the number of people forced from their homes—so-called climate refugees—contributes to social, economic, and political instability.

At the heart of climate change is carbon dioxide, or CO_2. A commonplace gas, CO_2 is necessary for life. Plants and trees take it in and give off oxygen; while humans and other creatures breathe in oxygen and exhale CO_2.

It is not breathing that is the problem, though; it is the increasing amounts of CO_2 and other gases emitted from our tailpipes and smoke stacks. As CO_2 enters the atmosphere, it traps heat, warming the earth. Like a blanket covering us on a cold winter's night, CO_2 provides natural insulation for the earth by trapping the heat of the sun in the earth's atmosphere.

This greenhouse effect is normal; but as we generate more and more CO_2 and other "greenhouse gases" such as methane while continuing to cut down the rainforests that are an important source of oxygen, the atmosphere warms beyond its normal range.

Your Carbon Footprint

A carbon footprint is the total amount of greenhouse gas emissions caused directly or indirectly by an individual, organization, or event. Reducing the size of our carbon footprint is a critical step in reining in the effects of climate change.

Many of the world's top scientists believe that reducing our carbon emissions 80 percent by the year 2050 is necessary to stabilize the earth's atmosphere and stave off the worst consequences of climate change,[5] which is just about two percent per year. If churches do their part, we can make a significant difference for God's creation. Many churches can reduce their carbon footprint by 10-25 percent in the first year with fairly simple changes.

Making those changes probably will not be hard to do, but first you have to calculate your current carbon footprint. While individuals can easily determine their carbon footprint, in this chapter you will learn how to calculate the carbon footprint of your church.

Choose the Type of Carbon Footprint to Use

In calculating your baseline carbon footprint, you have two options: brief or comprehensive. The brief calculation provides a general estimate of the amount of carbon dioxide your church's activities generate based on a few indicators such as utility bills, square footage of the church, commuting and travel practices of staff, types of computer servers used, the amount of packages shipped, and the amount of waste generated. One of the good things about the brief calculation is that you can skip parts of it. Even better, you can choose a "quick" option that asks simply for your state, industry, number of employees, and the square footage of your building. You will wind up with a goal baseline number that is easily obtained.

The comprehensive calculation provides a more accurate estimate based on the church's energy use, modes of transportation used by staff and members, types of goods and services used, and waste management practices. This calculation also includes a section on the kind of land the church owns. This figure will give you a lot of useful information.

Which option should you choose? Either one will do. The important thing is to have a starting point by which to measure your progress.

Collect Data

The following lists are adapted from information from Interfaith Power and Light. (You can find the full lists at *coolcongregations.com.*) To do a brief calculation for your church, you will need the following information:

- The kilowatt hours of electricity used per year or the square feet of your building
- The type of fuel used to heat your building (propane, natural gas, oil) and the gallons or cubic feet of fuel used per year or the square feet of your building
- Information about the servers used to support your computing (if applicable)
- The number and length of airline flights taken by staff for church-related travel. For help with this, check out the travel calculator at *nativeenergy.com.*
- Number of nights that staff spend in hotels on church-related travel
- The number of commuting church employees and the lengths of their commutes
- The amount of church waste generated and whether it is taken to the landfill or the incinerator

Remember, you can skip sections that are irrelevant or for which you are missing information.

For a comprehensive calculation designed specifically for houses of worship, you will need to collect more information, including:

- The average weekly worship attendance
- General attendance patterns of congregants
- General estimates of how people arrive at church (by car, bus, train, or non-motorized travel)
- Geographic setting (urban, suburban, rural)
- Transportation miles logged by staff for church-related work
- One year's worth of utility/energy bills
- Percentage of electricity generated by renewable sources
- Amount of trash generated at your church each week
- Amount of recycling done at church
- Money spent on different categories of goods and services per year, including paper and paper products, office supplies, cleaning supplies and services, furniture and fixtures, construction and renovations, food, apparel, linens and other textiles, printing and publishing, and other goods and services
- Information about your church's purchasing habits, for instance, do you purchase recycled, organic, sustainably produced items; or do you purchase standard items?
- Information about your church's land holdings
- Carbon offset information (if applicable)

Input Data

Several years ago, there were not many choices for calculating carbon footprints. Few people had access to the information necessary to crunch the data. Recently, however, online calculators have proliferated.

I have found the following two to be particularly helpful. You may be familiar with other ones you like better. Keep in mind that online resources can change without notice, so be prepared to answer slightly different questions than the ones noted in this chapter.

For the brief calculation, I recommend the calculator at Native Energy. Go to *nativeenergy.com,* and then click on the "Business" links.

For the comprehensive calculation, I recommend the Cool Congregations calculator (*coolcongregations.com*), designed specifically for houses of worship.

Save Your Figures

Once you have made your calculations, save a copy of the data you have input. Save a copy of results from the online calculations so that when you recalculate at year's end you will have much of the baseline information that you need. Practice going green here by printing out the results on the back of used paper or by saving a copy to your computer. Remember to turn off your computer, router, and printer when you finish.

Step 3. Make a Plan

"Truly I tell you, if you have faith the size of a mustard seed, you will say to this mountain, 'Move from here to there,' and it will move; and nothing will be impossible for you."
Matthew 17:20

Tasks
- Choose your approach
- Prioritize areas
- List resources
- Make a schedule

Now that you have calculated your carbon footprint, you are ready to make a plan for greening your church over the next year. You probably already have ideas about what you would like to accomplish. You may even have started making changes. Great! However, do not skip the planning step. This is your chance to map out the actions you will take and to think through the resources you will need to get the job done.

Choose Your Approach
Go Light Green
In "Areas of Focus," found in Part Two, implement several of "The Basics" from each of the twelve areas.

Every month, target a new area until you have touched each aspect of church life. At the end of twelve months, you will have brought a new environmental consciousness to your congregation. As interest continues to build, expect to see support for a deeper shade of green.

Go Medium Green

Incorporate the "The Basics," and then "Get Creative" by tackling more challenging options. By the end of twelve months, you will have noticeably shrunk your carbon footprint while expanding your commitment to sustainability.

Go Deep Green

Choose to "Go All Out" by implementing the most substantial changes available in each of the twelve areas of focus. Alternatively, focus all your efforts in one particular area, such as upgrading your heating and cooling system or overhauling your lighting system. If you go deep green in energy-related areas, you will notice a sizeable reduction in your carbon footprint. If you go deep green in worship, Christian education, or the grounds, you are preparing the soil for a deep shift in consciousness. Reductions in your carbon footprint will undoubtedly follow.

Go Checkerboard Green

Choose solutions from "The Basics," "Get Creative," and "Go All Out" for which your church has the most interest, money, and expertise, or for which you will encounter the least resistance. One church successfully built support by alternating quick achievements, such as buying fair-trade coffee, with bigger challenges, such as upgrading their heating and cooling system.

Prioritize Areas

Keeping in mind that this handbook is designed to guide you through a twelve-month process, decide which area of the church you want to focus on first. Rank the following in order of priority. Consult Part Two for more detailed ideas and information.

____	1.	Recycling
____	2.	Lighting
____	3.	Worship
____	4.	Electricity and Energy Efficiency
____	5.	Heating and Cooling
____	6.	Water
____	7.	Christian Education
____	8.	Vehicles and Travel
____	9.	The Kitchen
____	10.	The Office
____	11.	Missions
____	12.	Grounds

As you are planning, consider the finances, tools, equipment, people-power, expertise, and permissions that will be required to green each area.

List Resources

Now, list the resources you have available to you. Start by looking within your congregation. Do you have plumbers, electricians, contractors, educators, mechanics, or engineers among your members? Can you partner with the youth group, the women's or men's ministry, or the trustees? Investigate connections you can make to acquire the assets you will need such as equipment, tools, funding, and expertise. Be creative. Above all, pray! God can make a way where there is no way.

Network outside your church. Talk up what you are doing. You may find neighborhood groups or service organizations looking to take on worthy projects.

List your funding resources. These may come from the congregation, the denomination, or the larger community. Funds may also come from utility companies, grant-making bodies, or local organizations.

Perhaps the single most important resource you will need to green the church is internal support. Be sure to list the permission-givers and "power brokers" who are on your team. They will be invaluable not only to help with the politics and processes that are part of any church, but to secure the goodwill you will need as you green various areas of the church.

Make a Schedule

Make a list of the areas you plan to green. For each area, write down the actions you will take, the resources you will need, the resources available, the people who will be involved, and the expected date of completion. Note your funding sources as well as other pertinent information.

This handbook is set up to guide you through a twelve-month process, addressing one area per month. However, feel free to pick a timeframe and approach that will work for your church. Every situation is different. The important thing is to set achievable goals and a realistic schedule for meeting them.

Step 4. Take Action

The heavens are the LORD's heavens,
but the earth he has given to human beings.
Psalm 115:16

Tasks
- Follow the plan
- Track your progress
- Stay the course

Now that you have made a plan, you are ready to take action. Roll up your sleeves and enjoy! With each action you take, you are making a difference for the creation and future generations. Here are tips for how to proceed.

Follow the Plan

You have put considerable time into making a plan, so consult it regularly. Revise it as you go along, if needed. Once you get into the project, you will doubtless find that some things go smoother than expected, while others will involve unexpected challenges. Do not give up, and do not fret over making changes that need to be made.

Track Your Progress

Once you get started greening the church, keep track of your progress. Make note of how many incandescent bulbs you replace with CFLs. Keep track of how many exit signs get an LED makeover. Jot down how many pounds or boxes of junk mail you eliminate. Record the number of people who participate in actions such as a Bike to Church Sunday or a community garden. Statistics such as these will be helpful when you celebrate in Step 6.

Take pictures or video of your team in action. You can upload these to your church's website or Facebook page, show them in worship, embed them in newsletters, and use them as part of your closing celebration.

At the end of the year—or whatever period of time you have chosen—recalculate your carbon footprint. Compare it with your original calculation. Your initial goal may be to reduce your carbon footprint by ten or 20 percent. Remember the ultimate goal is an 80 percent reduction by 2050. It does not hurt to hit that goal sooner rather than later!

Stay the Course

Ground your work in prayer and Scripture. The Green Bible is an innovative resource to support you as you move into action. This New Revised Standard Version of the Bible uses green to highlight words about creation and justice.

Pace yourself. Greening the church is designed to be a twelve-month process (at least). It is a long-distance race, not a sprint. When you get stuck, look around to see who or what the Creator may have put in your path. Expect new support as you go along.

Glen Miles, senior pastor of Country Club Christian Church in Kansas City, Missouri, comments, "Our green team started as a result of complaints about the Styrofoam cups we were using. After hearing the complaints, I directed one of my staff to get a green team going. The team accomplished all sorts of stuff very quickly, but it took me about a year to decide to preach on it. As I was preparing to do so, I posted a question on my Facebook page to see which of my 600 'friends' were practicing environmental stewardship. I was floored at the positive response I got. People have been really open and receptive to my sermon series."

Step 5. Report Your Progress

And he said to them, "Go into all the world and proclaim the good news to the whole creation."

Mark 16:15

Tasks
- Consider your audience
- Choose methods of communication
- Compose messages
- Monitor responses
- Stay on point

When Jesus was born in order to bring salvation to the whole creation, God did not keep it a secret. Everyone was abuzz with the news. Cousin Elizabeth foretold it. Mary and Joseph knew. An angel of the Lord declared it to the shepherds. The heavenly host broke forth in praise to God. The Spirit whispered it to Simeon. Anna was in on it. Even the Magi had been tracking this development from afar. This news was too good to keep quiet.

Likewise, as you labor to conserve, protect, and honor the creation, do as the African American spiritual joyously recommends: "Go tell it on the mountain, over the hills and everywhere!" Do not keep this good news to your self. Tell it far and wide. Your church, your denomination, and your larger community will be vitally interested. Give them the opportunity to rejoice with you, and then be open to their responses.

Consider Your Audience

Some of your church's members will appreciate the environmental aspect of what you are doing. Others will appreciate the teamwork, fellowship, and excitement you are generating. Still others will be most interested in the bottom line. In your regular communications with church members, talk about all three.

"We met with some resistance," a long-time trustee recollected, "even though we were saving the church a great deal of money. I think it is because we neglected to keep people in the loop. They weren't sure what we were doing and why."

Through regular communication, you will gain more supporters. One team leader told me, "Our congregation is very supportive, even those who don't think environmental stewardship is all that important. Maybe it is because we're working with the children."

Choose Methods of Communication

There are many ways to communicate your message. I recommend choosing perhaps six of the following methods. Give updates at least once a month, if not more frequently, using a variety of verbal and written means.

Place a checkmark next to the methods of communication you will use. Make a plan to follow through.

___ Church newsletter
___ Website
___ E-mails
___ Announcements in worship (for example, Moment for Mission)
___ Notices in worship bulletin
___ Bulletin boards and displays
___ Banners
___ Messages from the pastor
___ Messages from the team
___ PowerPoint or video updates
___ Handouts
___ Newspaper announcements and stories
___ Skits
___ Requests for help
___ Denominational website or newsletter
___ Twitter, Facebook, MySpace, or other social networking sites
___ Stewardship announcements
___ Budget meetings
___ Signs throughout the church
___ Updates at church councils and boards
___ Updates in classes and small-group studies

Compose Messages

Make your progress reports joyful, interesting, and specific. Celebrate the church's faithful stewardship of money, energy, and God's beautiful creation. Include information about how others can join or support your group.

Monitor Responses

Communication is, of course, a two-way street. As you report your progress, you will get a variety of responses. Listen to what people say, and be sensitive to their concerns. As a team, decide how you will follow up on them.

Stay on Point

Remember to stay on point. One associate pastor confided to me, "Our Creation Care Team is persistent and consistent. Unfortunately, not all of our members are supportive. Sometimes we pastors get caught in the middle. But the task force gets the best hearing and makes the most progress when they stick with the Scriptural message of stewardship."

Do not give up. On the other hand, fighting or harsh words will not get you anywhere. Remember, prayer is a potent form of communication. Ask the Spirit who brought order out of chaos to bring order and understanding as you proceed with your plan to be good stewards of the creation.

Step 6. Celebrate in Worship

O sing to the LORD a new song;
sing to the LORD, all the earth.
                    Psalm 96:1

Tasks
- Review results and rewards
- Plan the service
- Give thanks

For twelve months or so, you have been greening your church. You have worked hard to increase the energy-efficiency of your facility, reduce your carbon footprint, raise awareness, and save money. Likely, you have witnessed a change in the attitude of your congregation. Doubtless, you have had a positive impact on the earth around you.

Now it is time to celebrate! Hold a special "Care of Creation" worship service. Do not skip this step. Celebration builds momentum, energizes people, and allows you to reflect on all you have accomplished. A celebration is also a good way to attract new supporters and resources.

Review Results and Rewards

Document and review the effect the project has had on your church's carbon footprint. Decide the best way to present those results during the worship service:

verbally, using a printed handout, or through a Power-Point presentation, a video, a skit, or other means.

In addition to reducing your carbon footprint, consider the other rewards that the church has experienced. Decide how to communicate and celebrate these rewards in the service. For example, the rewards might include:

- Better understanding of God's love for the whole creation
- Greater stewardship among members at home and at work
- Deeper fellowship
- Increased community awareness of your church
- Higher worship attendance
- Making new friends
- Forging new connections with the community
- Deeper worship life
- Stronger spirituality
- More congregational participation in the life of the church
- New Bible studies
- Newfound hope
- Ecumenical and interfaith connections
- Greater physical health
- Increased confidence
- Bigger visions for the future
- More money for mission work or other ministries
- Greater affinity with the rest of creation

Plan the Service

Decide where you will hold the service. Will it be indoors or outdoors? Will it be during regular worship or at another time?

Invite special guests from the neighborhood, denomination, nearby churches, interfaith organizations, vendors and suppliers, and environmental and scientific organizations. Remember elected officials and the press. If you plan on making this an interfaith service, invite members of other religions to be in on the planning from the beginning. Have you identified the group to whom you will "pay it forward" in Step 7? Invite them as well.

Choose your speaker. Will it be the pastor, your team leader, or another inspirational person? Perhaps you would like to have testimonies from members who have experienced a change in consciousness or awareness.

To enhance the program, include inspiring music. Also incorporate special rituals. If you have not done so already, plan to bless any new lighting, heating, and cooling systems. Bless gardens and compost piles. Bless the land your church sits on and the ecosystem of which you are part. Bless one another and the progress you have made. Plant trees to mark the greening of your church. Consult denominational resources for other ideas about the service.

Take a special offering to fund future energy-efficiency projects. Alternatively, if you have reduced your carbon footprint as much as you possibly can, then consider "offsetting" the rest of your carbon footprint by going carbon neutral. Contributions to companies such as Native Energy (*nativeenergy.com*) will help fund new alternative-energy projects.

As part of the celebration, host an open house. Give tours of the facility, pointing out the energy efficiencies now in place. Share other ways you have gone green that might not be immediately apparent. Then serve a special meal afterward that highlights local or organic food, fair-trade coffee, washable dishes and silverware, and plenty of time for relaxing and fellowship.

Give Thanks

Thank all those who contributed to the church's work. Most importantly, whether your celebration is large or small, simple or complex, give thanks to the Creator!

Step 7. Pay It Forward

How very good and pleasant it is
when kindred live together in unity!
Psalm 133:1

Tasks
- Select a partner
- Hold a get-to-know-you meeting
- Work together
- Stay connected
- Plan the next round

Now that you have greened your church, it is time to pay it forward. Be a green catalyst in your community.

Select a Partner

Partner or "eco-twin" with another church in your neighborhood, denomination, or community. If yours is a Protestant congregation, reach out to a Catholic or Orthodox congregation. Alternatively, consider partnering with a Native, Jewish, Buddhist, Muslim, Hindu, or other congregation.

Practicing stewardship of the creation is a great opportunity to make new connections. No matter our particular doctrines or beliefs, we all depend upon one earth, one water cycle, and one atmosphere to sustain us. Meeting the greatest moral challenge of our generation is the perfect opportunity to move out of old comfort zones and build new alliances.

One longtime church and environmental leader noted, "We're part of one of the most liberal Protestant denominations. We have traditionally worked among others like us. Now that the evangelicals are starting to embrace creation care, we are very hopeful about working together with them. We need to build a bridge of understanding."

Who should your church partner with? Ask for guidance in prayer. Also consider where you have existing connections. Think, too, about those who have shown an interest in your work over the past twelve months. Do you know other persons of faith who also want to build a sustainable future? If your pastor or priest belongs to a ministerial alliance or clergy cluster, natural connections can be made there.

Hold a Get-to-Know-You Meeting

Hold an initial meeting to get acquainted and begin planning. It would be ideal for each group to have its respective pastor, priest, rector, rabbi, imam, or spiritual leader present.

Start by holding a get-together in your house of worship, if both groups are comfortable there. Serve refreshments; but check first about possible dietary concerns, especially if you are working in an interfaith setting. Jews may keep kosher. Muslims do not eat pork. Mormons avoid caffeine. Buddhists and Hindus may be vegetarian. Also, double-check the day of the week that works best for everyone. Holidays, holy days, festivals, and sabbath schedules vary from group to group.

If you begin with prayer, invite your guests to offer a prayer as well. Do the same with Scripture or other teachings. Listen and learn. Each faith community possesses a wealth of ancient wisdom about human responsibilities toward the earth.

Work Together

Whether you choose to partner with a house of worship across town, across religious lines, or across cultural lines, you have much to share. Pass on your enthusiasm, experience, and wisdom. Share what worked and what did not. Show your guests around the building and grounds; point out where you made changes. Show them your utility bills, and let them see how it all adds up.

Next time, meet at their house of worship. Do a walk-through. Brainstorm together about what might work for them.

Stay Connected

Get together once a month or so for fellowship, support, and mentoring. Chances are that you will learn a great deal from one another. Pray for one another between get-togethers. If you begin this mentoring relationship before your Care of Creation celebration service, be sure to invite your partner congregation.

Above all, relax and enjoy! You are making a difference for creation in more ways than you know.

Plan the Next Round

By now, you have probably discovered that going green is an ongoing process, not a one-time event. Certainly, there is more to be done than can be accomplished in twelve months. As new innovations arise and new solutions come to the marketplace, you will find new ways to reduce your carbon footprint.

One longtime Christian affirmed, "Going green is a mindset; it is about changing your life. There will always be new things you have to consider. It is not like you do ten things and then you're done. It is an ongoing evolution."

She is right. I encourage you to go back to the beginning of this book and start again. This time, aim for a deeper shade of green. If you have covered "The Basics," then take the next step and "Get Creative." If you have been creative, then "Go All Out." If you have gone all out, do not stop there. Learn from what others are doing. Follow your instincts. Avail yourself of learning opportunities. Engage young people. Pass on all you have learned. Future generations are counting on you.

Part Two
Areas of Focus

1. The Resurrected Life: Recycling

Recycling gives plastic, glass, aluminum, paper, and other materials new life. It keeps precious natural resources out of landfills while protecting undisturbed sites from being industrialized. Recycling reduces water, air, and soil pollution, saves money, and provides jobs. It is the easiest creation-friendly act to take, and recycling is a biblical principle. You could say that resurrection is God's recycling plan. In Christ, our bodies and souls are gifted with eternal life. Through recycling, our natural resources are endowed with almost limitless possibilities.

The Basics

- Find out what kind of recycling facilities exist in your community. Do you have curbside recycling? drop-off bins at different locations? a recycling center?
- Discover what items can be recycled in your community. Items may include office paper, newspaper, magazines and catalogs, glass, plastic bottles, plastic bags, paper bags, steel cans, aluminum cans, computers and electronics, corrugated cardboard, paper board, fluorescent light bulbs, and compact fluorescent light bulbs (CFLs). Do not forget cell phones, eyeglasses, and ink cartridges, too.

- Is there a composting facility for biodegradable matter in your area? Find out if you can recycle food scraps and yard waste. Often these facilities allow you to reclaim wood chips or compost for your landscaping and gardening needs.
- Is there a "bottle bill" in effect in your city or state? If so, find out which kinds of glass and plastic bottles can be returned for a refund.
- Put labeled bins in the sanctuary for bulletins and inserts and bins in the office for paper, catalogs and magazines, phone books, cardboard, computers or electronics, and printer cartridges. Do not forget bins in the kitchen for glass, plastic, aluminum, and steel. If you are composting for a garden onsite, put out a special bin for food scraps.
- Communicate clearly and regularly about the location and purpose of the recycling containers.
- Designate a specific day on which recyclables will be put out for pickup or transported to drop off points.
- Rotate responsibilities for regular and consistent hauling of recyclables to your local recycling center. Include teens and children in this task.

Get Creative
- Sponsor a "Treasures in the Trash" art show with items made from recycled materials.

- Partner with a preschool or care facility in your area to double your recycling impact. Collect their recycling when you collect your own.
- Hold an aluminum can drive. Donate the proceeds to a favorite ministry, or sow the profits back into your Green Church ministry.

Go All Out

- Sign up with TerraCycle's fundraising campaigns to collect trash for "upcycling" into higher quality items (*terracycle.net*).
- Challenge another church to a friendly recycling competition. See which congregation can collect the most recyclables per capita or the greatest number of plastic bottles and aluminum cans.
- Using the National Recycling Coalition "Conversionator" (*nrc-recycle.org*), keep track of your monthly and yearly reductions in pollution and energy savings as you recycle. Make a display. Celebrate!
- Close the loop by purchasing recycled products, including paper, paper products, lumber, and carpet.

Challenge: At Home

Encourage everyone in your congregation to become a recycler. Even a small household can generate a wealth of recyclables. Hold a "Trash Challenge" to see which household can most reduce the amount they throw away. For every 15-gallon trash container you reduce, credit yourself 1,560 pounds of CO_2 saved from the atmosphere per year.[6] Don't forget to include the manse, rectory, or parsonage family in your efforts.

Sustainability in the Scriptures

> *To everything there is a season,*
> *and a time to every purpose under heaven:*
> *a time to be born, and a time to die;*
> *a time to plant, and a time to pluck up*
> *that which is planted.*
>
> *Ecclesiastes 3:1-2*
> *(King James Version)*

Did You Know?

Recycling adds up! Test your knowledge by reading the facts below to see how much you already know about recycling. Then find other recycling facts at *nrc-recycle.org* (click on "Consumers" and then "Recycling Calculator"), and discover just how much difference recycling can make.

- Every three months, Americans put enough aluminum in landfills to rebuild the entire commercial airfleet.

- Recycling an aluminum cans save enough energy to power a television for three hours.
- Americans throw away enough office paper each year to build a twelve-foot-high wall from New York to California.
- Recycling a stack of newspapers just three feet high saves one tree.
- Recycling one glass bottle saves enough electricity to power a 100-watt bulb for four hours.
- Five plastic soda bottles provide enough fiber to make one extra-large T-shirt, one square foot of carpet, or to fill one ski jacket.

We Did It!

Raised in a mission-oriented church in which environmental stewardship was often preached, Travis Dollar knew what his project would be when he set his sights on Eagle Scout. He would help the whole community go green by developing a recycling center in Skiatook, Oklahoma.

With help from the Reverend David Stephenson, pastor of First United Methodist Church of Skiatook, and the rest of his church family, Travis set out to make his goal a reality. Together with members of the church, he formed a recycling committee and began to raise awareness and money. In support of his efforts, the church included $1,500 in the budget to go toward the recycling center. Travis became so well-known among waste management personnel that he was invited to address a meeting that included waste management CEOs!

Travis's dream is now a reality. Skiatook's new tandem-axle recycling trailer accepts plastics #1 and #2 as well as aluminum cans in its several compartments. When it gets full, the items are hauled to the main recycling center near Tulsa, about 25 miles away. The trailer gets so much use that Skiatook is now considering expanding its capacities to include glass.

Meanwhile, Travis attained the rank of Eagle Scout and is enrolled as a mechanical engineering student at Oklahoma State University. Rev. Stephenson comments, "What's neat is that Travis's project has a lasting community-wide impact; it wasn't just for our little church. And isn't that what church is supposed to be?"

2. Let There Be Light: Lighting

Genesis tells us that the first thing God created was light. That Creation account underscores the primary importance of lighting in our lives and daily activities and is a great focus area for greening the church. According to Energy Star, lighting accounts for 20-50 percent of electricity consumption for a small business.[7] The changes you make in lighting systems will reduce your carbon footprint while saving energy and money.

The Basics
- Use natural daylight wherever possible.
- Do not overlight rooms. Too much light is as hard on the eyes as is too little light. Eliminate or turn off what you do not need.
- Post signs in each room to remind people to turn off lights when the room is not in use.
- Put a timer on outside lights. Program them to turn on only when needed.
- Replace incandescent bulbs with CFLs. Ninety percent of the energy used by an incandescent bulb is transformed into heat, not light. CFLs, by contrast, last ten times times longer and use 75 percent less energy than traditional incandescent bulbs.[8]

Get Creative

- Replace incandescent or CFL bulbs in exit signs with LEDs.[9]

- Replace older T-12 tube fluorescent bulbs (1" diameter) with newer, more efficient T-8s (1" diameter) or T-5s (⅝" diameter.) Long fluorescent bulbs should not go in the trash or landfill, as they contain hazardous materials that can leach out. Check with your local recycling site for options on disposal.

Go All Out

- Use LED lights instead of CFLs. When used about six hours per day, LEDs can last 22 years.[10]

- Install motion-sensitive lights in bathrooms, hallways, and outdoors. These sensors have to be able to "see" a person's movement, so do not install them behind doors, coat racks, or other barriers.

- Install a solar tube or tubular skylight. These highly refractive mini-skylights direct concentrated natural light indoors.

Challenge: At Home

As your incandescent bulbs burn out at home, replace them with CFLs. Choose "warm" bulbs to mimic the quality of light from incandescent bulbs and "cool" ones to mimic sunlight. CFLs work best in fixtures where the light is on at least fifteen minutes at a time. Look for special CFL bulbs designed for dimmer switches and recessed fixtures. If every home in America replaced their five most frequently used lights with CFL bulbs, our reduction in carbon emissions would be the equivalent of taking ten million cars off the road.[11] Do not forget to outfit the manse, rectory, or parsonage with energy-efficient lighting also.

Sustainability in the Scriptures

Then God said, "Let there be light"; and there was light. And God saw that the light was good; and God separated the light from the darkness. God called the light Day; and the darkness he called Night. And there was evening and there was morning, the first day.

Genesis 1:3-5

Did You Know?

Darkness is as important to our well-being as light, yet dark skies are increasingly rare. Brighter nights, brought on by increased human development and by unnecessary or poorly designed lighting, are throwing the creation out of whack. Light pollution silences the mating chorus of frogs and toads and causes birds to lose their way while migrating at night. When beaches are lit at night, sea turtles do not nest. Humans suffer as well: Increased rates of breast cancer in women may be linked to light pollution.[12] Astronomers have long known that seeing the glory of the heavens above requires turning out the lights below. If you need outside lights to be turned on at night, make sure they point downward and are motion-sensitive.

We Did It!

Pastor John Gorder has become a believer. He did not start off as a conservation-oriented pastor. Even though he was the General Secretary for the Joint Christian Ministry in West Africa, an interdenominational organization dealing with the impact of climate change on nomadic desert herders, the impact did not hit him personally until he wrestled with his own carbon footprint.

Gorder says, "My wife and I used a diesel generator to provide electricity when we were missionaries in the Central African Republic and Nigeria. We could see, hear, and smell the environmental impact. Between the fuel consumption, the pollution, and the noise—well, it was shocking."

His transformation continued when he came to pastor Augustana Lutheran Church of Hyde Park in Chicago in 1999. Seven years earlier, this congregation had been part of a pilot project in the Metropolitan Chicago Synod of the Lutheran Church (ELCA). With technical assistance from the Environmental Concerns Working Group of the Synod Justice Team, they had overhauled their lighting system.

First, outdated outdoor lighting fixtures were upgraded. Next, an outdoor light timer was replaced with a photo-sensor. Finally, standard incandescent bulbs in the sanctuary, hallways, and exit signs were replaced with CFLs.

Altogether, the congregation realized substantial savings. With an initial investment of $3,000, the lighting bills went down one-third, saving $1,200 per year. The overall return on investment was realized in 30 months. It took just six months to realize the return on investment for the exit signs. "No one makes that kind of money on Wall Street, short of being an inside trader," quipped James Schwab, chair of the Environmental Concerns Working Group and a member of the church.

Now, Gorder is a green pastor. He is quick to make connections between energy usage, global warming, and biblical notions of stewardship. He comments, "We're first-article people.[13] That means we are stewards of God's creation, which brings us incredible joy. We are sometimes oblivious to the joy creation brings to us. We just consume it. Now, in our parish, we deal with stewardship in our decision-making forums so that we can transform this information into our living. Knowing what I know now, my threshold of tolerance is decreasing when I see people leave lights on."

Gorder believes that doing serious work in the twenty-first century has to include motivating communities to understand creation and to take responsibility for protecting it. There is a gap between theory and practice. "Teachers, mentors, and practitioners are needed," he says. "Take it from me. I've seen myself transformed into a believer."

3. Praise the Lord: Worship

Worship is at the heart of the church and of creation. The psalmists write that the earth rejoices, the coastlands are glad, the trees clap their hands, and the heavens and earth praise God. Although we may not be able to hear it, when we gather to worship God we are joining our voices with the majestic choir of creation. Greening the church includes honoring, acknowledging, and advocating for our fellow creatures.

The Basics: Worship Service
- Music: So much of traditional hymnody lifts up the creation. Sing it!
- Paraments and banners: Creatively reflect your commitment to the whole of creation.
- Prayer: Focus on different aspects of the creation weekly, such as different animals, habitats, and greening efforts.
- Testimonies: Create a time to share insights about creation care and faith with the rest of the congregation.
- Children's sermon: Use this time to teach children about our interconnectedness with nature. Jesus told stories incorporating sky, sheep, goats, birds, flowers, mountains, and fields. So can we!

- Sermon: Encourage your pastor to preach a yearly series on our role as stewards of the creation.
- Baptism: Bless the waters that nourish the earth. Remember those in drought.
- Holy Communion: Use a chalice or reusable or compostable communion cups. Serve whole-grain organic bread. Remember to prepare a gluten-free alternative for those with gluten intolerance. Use organic wine or juice.

Get Creative: Outdoor Worship

- Institute an annual worship service in your local park; in the mountains; in the forest; or by a lake, river, or an ocean front. Incorporate time for quiet reflection. Listen for the choir of creation.
- Hold an outdoor baptism service at a nearby river or lake. Bless not only the newly baptized but the cleansing water that makes it possible.
- Host a Cowboy Church. These services connect Western stock culture with the gospel. Invent your own brand, and hold a service outdoors.

Go All Out: Special Services, Rituals, and Seasons

- Spring: Carbon-fast at Lent. Instead of giving up chocolate or donuts, reduce your energy consumption and carbon output. Put together a Lenten calendar with daily green suggestions so the whole congregation can "fast" together. For more information, go to *tearfund.org.*

- Summer: Bless the animals. Done outdoors, this delightful service, patterned after the loving commitment of Saint Francis of Assisi, can be followed up with a picnic, a hike, or a tour of a natural area.

- Fall: Bless the harvest. Invite gardeners, farmers, bakers, and hunters to bring in bounty to be blessed. Follow up with a feast. Acknowledge your interdependence with soil, water, air, forests, plants, and animals.

- Winter: Bless creation and the Incarnation. The incarnate presence of God means salvation for the whole cosmos, not only humanity. During Advent, connect the dots between the Incarnation and the redemption of all creation.

- Annually: Celebrate God's "rainbow covenant" with every living creature. Follow up with a congregational covenant with creation. Then live it out by continuing to go green.

- Incorporate the new four-week "Season of Creation" into your liturgical calendar. It highlights the work of God the Creator and the wonders of creation. For more information, go to *seasonofcreation.com.*

- Earth Day is April 22. Many churches designate the Sunday prior to it as the Festival of God's Creation. Special worship service helps may be available through your denomination. Also check out ideas from the National Council of Churches.

• Observe Earth Sabbath or Environmental Sabbath, a worldwide ecumenical day of reverence for the earth around June 5, World Environment Day. Gather with other congregations in your area to hold an interfaith service. Consider patterning your service after the United Nation's Environmental Sabbath Programme. For more information, go to *earthministry.org.*

Challenge: At Home

Include the creation in your daily prayers. Spend quiet time in nature to attune your soul to God. Bless elements of creation by name.

Sustainability in the Scriptures

> *Make a joyful noise to the LORD,*
> *all the earth.*
>
> *Psalm 100:1*

Did You Know?

Beeswax candles are more environmentally friendly than paraffin candles. Beeswax, naturally secreted from the bodies of honeybees, is a renewable source of light and heat, while paraffin is a petroleum-based product. Candles made of beeswax are also smokeless and produce no soot. They burn slower and longer than most paraffin-based candles. Their natural honey scent is the original aromatherapy for worship. Long considered sacred, beeswax candles are usually required for Catholic and Orthodox worship. Switching to beeswax candles is a simple step you can take to green your church.

We Did It!

All Souls Interfaith Gathering in Shelburne, Vermont, is not going green. They already are and have been for a long time.

Since its inception in 1999, this community of worshipers has been convinced that the earth is God's most extraordinary creation. The members already sense a connection between the earth and spirituality, so it is a natural move for them to honor and worship the Divine by caring for the creation.

From the Environmental Speaker Series, in which people from all walks of life address the congregation, to the Celtic Mass of Peace, which was recorded in their sanctuary, the message of mutual interdependence with the earth is made clear at almost every service. Innovative rituals, adapted for this intentionally interfaith congregation, add to the message. Once a year they celebrate a Flower Communion. Another time of year, they celebrate a Blessing of the Waters. The first ritual speaks of rebirth, while in the second ritual "we see that all the water is one, as people are one," explains Mary Abele, the founding minister of All Souls. Every week, a meditation is offered that focuses on healing for the world.

Abele, a soft-spoken but passionate voice for spirit and nature, is the empowering force behind this congregation of 70 souls. "I was raised near Walden Woods in Concord, Massachusetts, the setting that inspired Henry David Thoreau," Abele reminisces. "It was normal to walk miles in the woods. For me, respect for nature has always been a part of my being."

Respect for nature surrounds the worshipers at All Souls. It is not just the worship; it is the building itself. Constructed in 2007, it makes use of many earth-friendly features. Local maple trees, downed after an ice storm, were used in the construction of the sanctuary. The flooring is made of sustainable bamboo. A nearby artesian well cools water used for air conditioning, while a wood-pellet stove heats the building.

Most noticeable, however is the huge bank of windows in the sanctuary that looks west over Lake Champlain to the Adirondack Mountains. With a service at five o'clock in the afternoon, people can watch the sun set and see rainstorms coming across the lake. "It is absolutely stunning," said Abele. "We've got the outdoors practically coming inside."

She adds, "My goal is to empower people. I'm a big believer that there are all sorts of ways you can change things for the better. For instance, plant a certain flower and you get butterflies."

Take a close look at the All Souls Interfaith Gathering that Abele has nurtured, and you can see that same positive principle in action.

4. Jesus Saves:
Electricity and Energy Efficiency

Electricity makes the world go 'round. Chances are that it powers everything from your worship service to the preschool to the pastor's office. Despite advances in renewable energy production, most electricity in the United States is generated from coal-fired plants. Natural gas comes in second, followed by nuclear power.[14] Energy that is generated from coal and natural gas puts greenhouse gases into the atmosphere: CO_2 for the former and CO_2 and methane for the latter. Using less electricity slows down global warming, saves money, and provides more resources to engage a church's primary mission. When it comes to going green, energy conservation is the biggest plus there is.

The Basics
- Get an energy audit of your facility. Contact your local utility company to see if they will conduct one.
- Turn off lights and electronics when not in use. Place signs on or near equipment to remind people.
- Make sure equipment is all the way off. If the power cord has a boxy transformer for a plug-in or if lights are still visible on the appliance when it is off, then it is using "phantom" or standby power. When tasks

are finished, unplug the item or turn off the surge protector or power strip that it is plugged into. Standby power can account for almost ten percent of your church's total power consumption.[15]

- Do a walk-through of your church. Is the freezer next to the heating vent? Is a radiator next to an entryway? Rearrange the space for better efficiency.

Get Creative

- Replace aging appliances, especially refrigerators and freezers. A new refrigerator certified by Energy Star will use half as much energy as those made before 1993.[16]

- Replace your hot-water heater with an on-demand, tankless water heater. If your church uses 41 gallons or less of hot water daily, on-demand water heaters can be 24-34 percent more energy efficient than conventional storage tank water heaters. If your church uses 86 gallons or more per day, on-demand water heaters will be 8-14 percent more energy-efficient.[17]

- Remember to check into recycling options for major appliances before discarding them.

Go All Out

- Harness the wind: If you have average annual wind speeds of at least ten miles per hour, if utility-supplied electricity is 10-15 cents per kilowatt hour, and if it is not too expensive to hook up to your local grid, then small-scale wind power can reduce your electricity bills by 50-90 percent.[18]

- Soak up solar power: Solar power works best in the Southwestern United States. Photovoltaic cells actively produce power from the sun, while forms of passive solar power heat up water and other surfaces.

- Dig into the earth: Geothermal power provides steady, even heat from beneath the earth's surface for heating, cooling, and hot water.[19] Expect utility bills to be 30-40 percent lower than if you were using regular heat pumps. Although initially expensive to install, geothermal power provides a return on investment in five to ten years.

Challenge: At Home

Turn off all lights at home when they are not in use. Check your home appliances, including stove, refrigerator, freestanding freezer, microwave, dishwasher, washer, dryer, water heater, furnace, fans, air conditioner, television, computer, and other electronics for a blue-and-white Energy Star designation, awarded for energy efficiency. Wherever possible, unplug what you are not using. Consider replacing inefficient models with more efficient ones. Do not forget to check the manse, rectory, or parsonage as well. Investing in energy efficiency saves money in the long run.

Sustainability in the Scriptures

*May the God of steadfastness and encouragement
grant you to live in harmony with one another,
in accordance with Christ Jesus.*

Romans 15:5

Did You Know?

The US Department of Energy recommends that you turn off your computer monitor if you are going to be away from it for at least twenty minutes.[20] If you will be away from your computer for two hours, then turn off the monitor and the CPU. The less time your computer is on, the longer it will last. Although there is a brief power surge when turning on a computer, its less than the energy required for long periods of use. Alternatively, you can program newer computers to go into sleep mode when not in use, requiring less energy than required to run it than when "awake." A screen saver is not the same thing as sleep mode and may draw more energy. Newer LCD screens do not need screen savers to protect them.

We Did It!

By all accounts, the sanctuary of First United Methodist Church in Laramie, Wyoming, looks like an upended ark, with the prow piercing the sky. It is eye-catching—so are the heating bills that go with it. Not good. While the people of the church are naturally warm, the building is not. In fact, the whole building seems to have been constructed with energy *in*efficiency in mind.

In the winter, church services were moved from the sanctuary to the warmer education building. However, that building was not much warmer. The cinder-block walls with external brick overlay were not insulated. With heating radiators mounted on the outside walls, natural gas-powered heat easily escaped, and utility bills soared.

Enter Dave Earnshaw. With this engineer, environmentalist, and long-time church member at the helm, there was no place to go but up. Layers of insulation were added to the sanctuary. Next, foam insulation coated with reflective aluminum was installed between the hot water radiators and the cinder block walls of the education building. Dial thermostats were replaced with seven-day programmable thermostats. "To really get value out of programmable thermostats," Earnshaw explains, "they must be programmed weekly. You can't just set 'em and forget 'em. Every Sunday night, one of us has to make the rounds and set the thermostats for the following week."

Quilted window coverings made by volunteers were used to cover the windows in the education building. Additionally, two radiators were moved to better heat the narthex. Overall, it is amazing how much cozier the building has become.

While there is still work to be done, the results have been impressive. Over the course of 20 months, the church saved $7,214 in natural gas costs, while preventing 63,551 pounds of carbon dioxide from entering the atmosphere. That is the equivalent of taking more than five cars off the road every year! That figure does not include the savings that accrue from upgrading the lighting systems.

Long-term plans include replacing all windows with energy-efficient windows, insulating the outside of the building, and figuring out how to insulate the gorgeous 750-square-foot stained-glass rose window that adorns the sanctuary wall. With Dave Earnshaw in charge, the sky is the limit!

5. To Everything There Is a Season: Heating and Cooling

Heating and cooling are among the largest energy uses in a house of worship. They also contribute most to a church's energy costs. Making changes here will allow you to experience big savings in energy and money while reducing your carbon footprint. Follow these simple practices to keep the building warmer in winter and cooler in summer as you reduce your church's contributions to global warming.

The Basics
- Seal up air leaks by caulking around electrical openings, cracks in the wall, and at the junction of floors and walls. Install weatherstripping around doors and windows. Seal the heating and cooling ducts. This step alone can improve energy efficiency by 20 percent.
- After sealing leaks, then add insulation.
- Replace air filters monthly, especially during periods of heavy use.
- Perform annual or seasonal maintenance on heating and cooling systems.
- Have your HVAC system evaluated. If it has been improperly installed, you may be losing efficiency.

- Install programmable thermostats, then set them to heat and cool automatically when the church is being used. In colder months, set daytime temperatures at 65-68 degrees and nighttime temperatures at 55-58 degrees. In warmer months, set daytime temperatures at 78 degrees. Do not cool the building at night if it is unoccupied.[21]

Get Creative

- Plant trees to serve as wind blocks and to shade your building. Keep buildings at the desired temperatures by using window coverings such as quilted curtains, awnings, blinds, draperies, reflectivity films, insulated panels, window screens, overhangs, shades, shutters, and storm panels.
- Install ceiling fans to circulate cool air during warm weather and warm air during cool weather.
- In dry climates, consider installing an evaporative cooler instead of air conditioning.
- In moderate climates, consider a heat pump that will heat and cool your facility. Heat pumps move already existing heat indoors in cool months instead of generating it or outdoors in warm months instead of cooling it.[22]
- If your HVAC system is not performing or is older than ten years, consider replacing with a model certified by Energy Star.

Go All Out

- Replace old windows with panes that are certified by Energy Star. Low-energy glass can reduce heat loss dramatically.
- See if you can install clear glass or plastic storm windows over stained-glass windows to trap heat. Be careful, as this might also trap moisture, thereby damaging the lead. Check with a professional before proceeding.
- Install an active solar-heating system.
- Install geothermal heat wells to make use of the earth's heat.

Challenge: At Home

Start by sealing up leaks around doors and windows. Add insulation where needed. Install programmable thermostats. Make sure you are not overheating or over-cooling. Replace old doors and windows with new ones certified by Energy Star. Check with your power company about an energy audit for your home. Remember to green the manse, rectory, or parsonage as well.

Sustainability in the Scriptures

As long as the earth endures,
>   *seedtime and harvest, cold and heat,*
summer and winter, day and night,
>   *shall not cease.*

Genesis 8:22

Did You Know?

You can get help in figuring out how to make your church more energy efficient. Energy Star, a division of the Environmental Protection Agency, works with all types of congregations to provide free, unbiased advice. To get started, go to *energystar.gov*. Then research the financial incentives, rebates, and policies available for purchasing energy-efficient appliances and installing sources of renewable energy at The Database for State Incentives for Renewables and Efficiency (*dsireusa.org*). This site will give you state-by-state information.

We Did It!

The Reverend Karen Chalk, a chemist turned priest, arrived just in time at the Anglican Parish of St. Andrew and St. Mark in Dorval, a borough of Montreal. Hydro Québec, the green-energy supplier for this northeastern Canadian province, had withdrawn its preferred electricity rate for churches. It looked as though the church would have to switch completely to oil. Financially and environmentally it would be a devastating move.

Chalk recalls, "To spend more and buy something that was poisoning us—oh, no; that was no good. What were we going to do? It seemed horrifying."

In a serendipitous move, the former mayor of Dorval, also a member of the church, encouraged Chalk to look into geothermal alternatives, which the city had successfully undertaken. "We put a little team together to research it, including an engineer," says Chalk. "We found a company we were comfortable with, and we went for it. It helped that at the general meeting I could explain it to my congregation."

They tore out their oil furnaces and installed eight geothermal wells, each almost 500 feet underground. U-shaped vertical loops were inserted into the wells, carrying an antifreeze heat-transfer fluid. Inside the church, geothermal heat pumps would extract heat from the fluid as it circulated from the vertical loops to the pumps and back again. Because the earth maintains a steady heat of about 60 degrees Fahrenheit, their geothermal system would heat the church in winter and cool it in the summer. When the month-long installation was complete, Chalk led the congregation in a festive blessing of the geothermal wells.

Indeed, the system has been a big blessing. It has reduced the church's heating costs by about 40 percent, a significant savings for any church, but especially for this aging congregation of 80-85 worshipers.

In the beginning, the congregation was not sure they were willing to risk it. The installation would cost about $160,000, a frightening prospect. However, a recently sold rectory made the initial investment possible. Chalk recalls, "We were making $7,000 a year on our nest egg. That seemed like a lot. We realized that the savings from geothermal would add up to even more than that." Indeed, the first year alone they saved about $23,000 in heating costs while averting the use of 33,000 liters (8,718 gallons) of heating oil.

There were unexpected bonuses as well. For the first time ever, summer worship attendance rose 25 percent with worshipers from all over the city. "We're now the only church in Montreal with air conditioning," a delighted Chalk explains.

This is a time of great optimism for the Anglican Parish of St. Andrew and St. Mark. "The future of our church was always on our minds," says Chalk. "We're doing repairs and renovations that should have been done 15 years ago. This has created real hope for us; we are now confident about our future."

What is next for this congregation? Chalk responds without missing a beat: "Solar panels for generating electricity. What we don't use, we'll sell back to the grid." It is still a dream for this parish, one that may take ten years to realize; but that is just about the time the geothermal system will have paid for itself. For a visionary priest unafraid of technology, Karen Chalk is confident that their dream will come true.

6. The Wells of Salvation: Water

Water plays an important role throughout the Bible. The website for the National Council of Churches' Eco-Justice Programs notes: "In the Bible, rivers are mentioned 258 times, streams 24 times, and water 714 times."[23] Undoubtedly, these frequent references have something to do with a desert environment; but no matter where you live, water is precious. The Christian symbol of renewal and rebirth, water is absolutely essential for all forms of life. Not only are our bodies mostly water, so is the surface of the earth. Protecting and conserving this life-giving element is an important part of greening your church. Every drop counts.

The Basics

- Fix leaky faucets, nozzles, and pipes in bathrooms and the kitchen. Remember to check outside water spigots for drips and leaks.
- Test irrigation systems to ensure that all sprinkler heads are working properly and are pointed in the right direction. Remember to water the ground, not the sidewalks or parking lot! Better yet, install drip irrigation or hoses that are imbedded in the ground. Choose plants that need little or no watering.

- Water in the cool of the morning or evening to reduce evaporation. Avoid watering on windy days.

- Retrofit your toilets. Place one or two plastic bottles filled with an inch or two of sand or pebbles inside your toilet tank. This will reduce the amount of water flushed away.

- Do not let water run while washing hands, preparing food, or washing dishes.

- Refrigerate water for drinking instead of letting the tap run until it gets cold. This can save gallons of water.

- Compost food scraps instead of using a garbage disposal. You will save on water and potential septic tank problems down the line.

- Set the hot-water temperature at 120 for comfortable hand-washing temperatures. You may need higher temperatures for dishwashers.

- Insulate your water heater if it was manufactured before 1989.

- Replace aging water heaters with high-efficiency units that are certified by Energy Star.

Get Creative

- Use baptismal water to irrigate outside plants. Better yet, plant a drought-resistant tree for each person baptized. Trees conserve water.

- Install a rain barrel to collect water for outdoor uses. This keeps water in underground aquifers for the future.

- If local codes allow it, divert "gray water" from sinks and showers to water lawns, gardens, and trees.

Go All Out
- Do not use or promote the use of bottled water. Quite often it is no cleaner or safer than tap water.[24] At church functions, serve water in pitchers. Filter the water if possible.
- Install controls that turn bathroom faucets off automatically.
- Install low-flow toilets.
- Plant a rain garden. Water it using a rain barrel or stormwater runoff from your parking lot.
- Design a bioswale—a wide, shallow ditch—at the edge of the parking lot to remove silt and pollution from surface water runoff. Plant with buffalo grass or other slow-growing grass.

Challenge: At Home

Fix leaks, drips, and worn washers. Do not let the water run when washing dishes, preparing food, or brushing your teeth. Take showers, not baths. Drink tap water, not bottled water. Use a reusable water container made of lined stainless steel. Apply these water saving strategies at the manse, rectory, or parsonage as well.

Sustainability in the Scriptures

With joy you will draw water
from the wells of salvation.[25]
Isaiah 12:3
(New International Version)

Did You Know?

Almost three-fourths of the earth is covered in water, so it seems as if there is plenty of water to go around. However, most of the water on the planet, about 97 percent, is in the oceans. Of the remaining three percent of earth's water, about 69 percent of that is frozen in the polar ice caps and glaciers. That leaves a small amount to nourish the rest of creation, making the conservation of water extremely important. Drips from a leaking faucet can waste 20 gallons of water per day![26]

We Did It!

The Reverend Angela Shepherd, a child of the 1970's, was deeply affected by the first energy crisis. "I've always been one who has cared for the environment and nature," she explains. So it seemed a natural opportunity to combine her love of nature with her Christian faith when Anne Pearson, a local environmentalist, approached her about installing a rain garden at St. Philips Episcopal Church in Annapolis, Maryland.

With grants from the Chesapeake Bay Foundation and Unity Gardens, the church was able to proceed.

Now St. Philips has a water-conserving rain garden. This twenty-foot-wide oval garden sits in a bowl at the base of the sloped parking lot. When it rains, the water naturally courses down the parking lot and collects in the garden. Most years, that means the garden does not need to be watered at all.

This lovely garden, full of bee balm, iris, and other native plants, attracts monarch butterflies, yellow swallowtail butterflies, and a variety of birds. Deer and rabbit can be seen on the grounds, too. Senior citizens, who live at the nearby assisted-living center, also visit the garden. They and other groups that use the church now enjoy relaxing on the beautiful granite benches that grace the garden. The space also includes an altar, making it conducive to outdoor worship.

The rain garden has inspired creativity as well. The grants included funds to work with a potter, so St. Philips held an intergenerational workshop to create squares of clay now positioned around the granite benches. These handcrafted blocks contain sacred words and pictures that bless the area.

Shepherd, or Mother Shepherd, as she is known by her active parish, is the first female rector in this historically African American congregation. Now in her tenth year, she is working on institutionalizing environmental change so that it sticks. She is determined that the current wave of earth awareness—unlike during the first energy crisis, which promised change but did not deliver—will involve permanent transformation.

In a way, that is exactly what the church's new garden accomplishes. Instead of rainwater being diverted into the sewer system and away from the area it was intended to irrigate, the rain garden allows it to gently filter back into the ground, replenishing the earth even as it creates a thing of beauty.

Conservation, beauty, nature, and community—with these fine attributes, St. Philips expects the rain garden to be around for years to come.

7. Raise Up a Child: Christian Education

Begin now to teach children the connection between faith and the environment—indoors and out. Childhood is a time of innate spirituality, creativity, and learning. By design, time spent in nature draws out these qualities in children. Yet it is no longer a given that young people will play or spend much time outdoors. Returning children to nature, to cultivate a sense of awe and wonder, can be an important part of Christian education. Connecting the creation to the Creator magnifies the learning experiences of children.

The Basics
- Include children in the process of greening your church.
- Use Bible studies and curricula that teach environmental stewardship as part of one's faith commitments. Check out *Green Church: Caretakers of God's Creation* (for children) and *Burst: Green Church* (for youth), a pair of six-week studies that go with the adult six-week study *Green Church: Reduce, Reuse, Recyle, Rejoice!*
- Plant seeds and trees as part of Sunday school education and watch them grow.

- Send children to summer church camp where they can connect the Creator and the creation.

Get Creative

- Help children and teens design plays or skits that can be performed on Earth Day Sunday or as part of a stewardship focus.
- Design a vacation Bible school that takes children outside. Give them time for play, reflection, and outdoor exploration. Tell a Bible story or parable outside. Help young people make a connection between the words and the world around them.
- Take children on nature walks. Focus on streams, birds, trees, flowers, clouds, bugs, animals, or other natural features that are nearby.

Go All Out

- Create an outdoor play environment on church grounds for use by Sunday school classes and the surrounding neighborhood. Incorporate trees, sandboxes, and birdhouses to observe wildlife, and paths and bridges to explore interesting natural features.
- Clean up and green up an unused or abandoned area in your neighborhood as a child-to-child outreach from your church. Engage the children in your church to create a green play area for other neighborhood children.

- Put together a church camping weekend. Design a worship service that incorporates readings from Genesis and the Psalms as well as silent meditation time. Focus on caring for the creation as a way of loving God.
- Design a summer retreat in which adults mentor young people in the vital connection between spirituality and nature.

Challenge: At Home

Take a sabbath from the computer and the television. Spend time outdoors. Garden, hike, fish, camp, hunt, go bird-watching, enjoy nature walks. Take children, grandchildren, and other children with you. Introduce them to the wonders of nature. Breathe deeply. Relax. Enjoy!

Sustainability in the Scriptures

Train children in the right way
and when old, they will not stray.
Proverbs 22:6

Did You Know?

Spending time outside in unstructured play is critical to children's growth and development. Playing outdoors increases confidence, inner peace, and a sense of wonder and awe. It reduces depression, obesity, and ADHD.

Despite the benefits, children are spending less and less time outdoors. By age eight, they often have greater familiarity with video-game characters than with wildlife species. Many of these kids experience "Nature Deficit Disorder," an unofficial diagnosis that describes the social, physical, intellectual, and spiritual costs of too much time spent indoors. Read *Last Child in the Woods: Saving Our Children From Nature Deficit Disorder,* by Richard Louv, for more information.

We Did It!

Krista Kimble had been a member of B.U.G.S. (Better Understanding of Green Stewardship) since it began. B.U.G.S. was a homegrown environmental stewardship program of the Church of the Brethren in Manassas, Virginia. As Kimble grew more involved, however, she realized that something was missing: children.

Using her skills as a mother, educator, Girl Scout leader, and journalist, Kimble designed a curriculum for children, called Jr. B.U.G.S. that complements the adult activities. "It sounds hokey," Kimble ventured, "but I literally dreamed about Jr. B.U.G.S." When she awoke, she got to work.

Now, in its third year, Jr. B.U.G.S attracts a core group of ten to twelve children, from kindergarten to fifth grade. They get together for sessions in the spring and fall to learn about how the earth works. Their interest is rewarded with a variety of badges, such as Burt Beetle for recycling, Lucy Ladybug for gardening, Wanda Worm for composting, Benny Bee for pollination, and Darla Dragonfly for water resources. The Bible-based curriculum also includes Scripture verses, hands-on learning, fun facts, and service projects.

"Our church has always been front-and-center on green things," Kimble said proudly. "In 1999, we adopted a Green Resolution." By adopting the resolution, the Virginia congregation of more than 200 members decided to compost leftovers from church dinners, to garden and give away the food, to use green cleaning supplies, and to dispose of trash responsibly. Kimble adds, "It seemed a natural thing to do to include the children."

The children's involvement has brought even more adults on board. While parents help out with support and snacks, members with special skills are invited to share their knowledge with the Jr. B.U.G.S. "We had a master gardener teach the kids about plants that attract pollinators," Kimble explains. "A man who keeps honeybees showed the kids the inside of a hive."

The children enjoy what they are learning. Kimble reports, "I always get the children asking me when we're going to start. Even though I'm crazy busy, it makes me happy that the children are so excited."

Each year, the children take a Jr. B.U.G.S. pledge to learn more about the earth that God created, to explore ways of being better stewards of the environment, to help make the world a better place, and to teach others to do the same. With the support of her congregation, Karen Kimble is transforming that pledge into practices that will last a lifetime.

8. What Would Jesus Drive? Vehicles and Travel

No, Jesus did not drive a car; but this question, first posed by the Evangelical Environmental Network, makes a good point. Does it matter if we drive a Honda or a Hummer? Would Jesus care? My bet is that the one who taught us to love our neighbor as ourselves would choose a vehicle with the lightest impact on creation. On average, every mile we drive puts about a pound of CO_2 into the air.[27] In a car-driven society, that adds up quickly. Here are a number of ways to green your ride, while showing love for your neighbors.

The Basics
- Service church vehicles regularly. Keep the tires inflated to recommended pressures to improve gas mileage.
- Unload extra weight to improve gas mileage.
- Do not be a lead-foot. Driving at 55 miles per hour saves fuel and reduces greenhouse gas emissions.
- Stack meetings, rehearsals, and events where possible to reduce driving time and carbon emissions.
- Arrange neighborhood carpools. Arrange for one van to pick up people instead of everyone driving their cars to church.

- Combine trips. Do not hop in the car every time you think of something to do. Make a list of places you need to go first, and then plan accordingly.
- If you have a choice of vehicles to drive, choose the most fuel-efficient one for your needs.

Get Creative
- Use teleconferences or videoconferencing when meeting in person is not necessary.
- Design a Bike to Church Sunday. Encourage as many individuals and families to bike to church to reduce carbon emissions. Provide bike racks.
- Institute a low-carbon Sunday. Once a month, encourage church members to reduce their travel carbon footprint. Ask drivers to carpool, walk, ride bikes, or take public transportation. Calculate the amount of CO_2 emissions you have averted by figuring that an average of one pound of CO_2 is generated per mile driven.

Go All Out
- Chart your congregational carbon footprint. Calculate the amount of carbon dioxide each member generates when driving and flying each year. First, find out the miles-per-gallon rating for your vehicle at *fueleconomy.gov*. Then, use the travel calculator at *nativeenergy.com* to figure how many tons of

CO_2 you have generated. (This site also provides tools for calculating air travel.)

- Set a congregational goal to reduce driving emissions by ten percent per year by driving less and driving more efficiently.
- Tithe your CO_2. Ask church members to tithe $10 per ton of CO_2 emissions generated from driving and flying.
- Challenge your church members to trade up to a more fuel-efficient vehicle.
- Convert the church van to biodiesel.

Challenge: At Home

Incorporate the basics into your home life. Drive less, and walk and bike more. Carpool and use public transportation where possible. Seriously consider whether you need an SUV or pickup truck for your daily needs. Consider the impact of your driving habits on the rest of the world. Drive a more fuel-efficient vehicle.

Sustainability in the Scriptures

You shall love your neighbor as yourself.

Matthew 22:39

Did You Know?

Like Hummers, SUVs were originally designed as military combat vehicles that could be driven off-road when necessary. However, in the civilian world, less than five percent of SUVs ever leave the road.[28] Most of them are purchased because of perceived safety advantages. Studies show, however, that the more fuel-efficient vehicles actually have a better safety record. The International Council on Clean Transportation reports, "Some of the safest vehicles have higher fuel economy, while some of the least safe vehicles driven today—heavy, large trucks and SUVs—have the lowest fuel economy."[29] That is good news for the climate, since transportation is responsible for a third of all global warming pollution in the United States.[30] Next time you buy a vehicle, consider the hypothetical question, "What would Jesus drive?"

We Did It!

Jack Twombly does not ride his bike much anymore. At 87, he has slowed down a bit; but that has not stopped this passionate, articulate, retired professor of electrical engineering from helping his church's Creation Care Task Force organize their regular Bike to Church Sunday.

Once a year, people from all over town bicycle to church at the First Presbyterian Church of Boulder, Colorado. In return, they are treated to a delicious buffet breakfast in the church's courtyard. "So far," Twombly reports, "we have been blessed with beautiful weather each time. It is great to see whole families show up on their bikes."

The breakfast is not just for those who arrive on two wheels. Those who walk, skateboard, carpool, or take public transportation are also welcomed. "We're trying to discourage people from driving alone to church," says Twombly. Noticeably absent at the breakfast are Styrofoam cups and plastic silverware.

This spring event, advertised well in advance, draws a good turnout. Anywhere from 200-300 people participate, which adds up to a lot of bike shorts in the pews. A committed group of eight to ten task force members are at the heart of this effort. Carl Hofmann, one of the associate pastors of this 2,000-member congregation, is an ardent cyclist and strong advocate. That day, even he wears bike shorts. "It is a great day for fellowship," comments Hofmann. "It has deepened our sense of community. It has also brought new members to the Creation Care Task Force."

Bike to Church Sunday is an exciting breakthrough at First Presbyterian. "Our church is fairly conservative," says Twombly. "Even now, care of creation is something of a tough sell here. Scripturally, we are on solid ground—economically, too; but people don't seem to understand the need for a wiser use of energy."

Yet Twombly does. His professional background in electrical engineering has well-acquainted him with the connection between energy issues and the health of creation. That is why he founded the task force some years ago and has served for over a decade as his presbytery's Stewardship of Creation enabler.

Even in the face of discouragement Twombly is persistent. He has good reason to be. "I have 21 grandchildren," he says. "Twenty-one! They're my biggest motivation. I have strong apprehensions about the kind of world they're entering as they go out of childhood into adulthood. As long as I can, I'll do whatever I can to ensure a better world for them."

9. Bread of Life: The Kitchen

Every Sunday we offer people the bread of life, yet our fellowship hour boasts some of the unhealthiest practices of the church. Taking a close look at how and what we eat at church is an important part of going green and so is maintaining and sustaining good health. Dealing with unhealthful food, toxic cleaning supplies, and wasteful practices are simple ways of deepening our commitment to greening the church.

The Basics

- Encourage the use of mugs instead of paper or Styrofoam cups at coffee hour. Create a wall of mugs that can be used and reused. Be sure to include mugs for guests.
- Use the "good" dishes and flatware at church dinners instead of throwaways such as Styrofoam, plastic or foam plates, and plastic utensils. Alternatively, ask people to bring their own table service for meals.
- Use dishtowels instead of paper towels and maybe even cloth napkins instead of paper napkins. When using paper, make it recycled.

- Wherever possible, buy organic foods. Pesticides harm the health of growers and consumers; and they taint soil, water, and air.
- When eating fish, choose species that are not being overfished. For more information, go to *monterey bayaquarium.org*.
- Purchase and serve fair-trade coffee, tea, and chocolate. Fair-trade items emphasize responsible stewardship of the land and provide a good living for the growers. Shade-grown coffees, planted and harvested under the forest canopy, are particularly bird-friendly. For more information, go to *coffeereview.com*.
- Compost leftover food.
- Reuse plastic bags as garbage can liners. When purchasing new plastic bags, look for ones made of recycled plastic. Choose those with a high post-consumer waste (PCW) content.
- Look carefully at the cleaning agents you are using. Many contain harmful or toxic ingredients. Purchase and use environmentally-friendly cleaning agents.
- Refrain from buying antibacterial soaps. Generally, plain soap and water are as effective. Antibacterials seem to cause more problems than they solve.[31]
- Try toilet paper and paper towels made of recycled paper.
- Just say no to commercial air fresheners; many contain phthalates which are linked to human health

problems. Fresh air, sunshine, fans, and baking soda in the bottom of a garbage can provide natural air freshening.[32]

Get Creative

- Make your own green cleaning supplies.
- Experiment with natural sachets for bathrooms that make use of essential oils or natural herbs and spices.
- Establish a scent-free zone in the sanctuary to accommodate those with asthma and allergies.
- Try holding meat-free potlucks. Bovines such as beef, buffalo, lamb, and goat produce methane, a greenhouse gas that is twenty-three times more potent than CO_2.[33] Choose poultry, grain, beans, and eggs to achieve a lower carbon footprint.
- Make your own communion bread out of organic, whole-grain flour.

Go All Out

- Ask church members to observe one meat-free day per week and to limit seafood consumption to species that are not being overfished.
- Hold cooking classes to help people rediscover the art of cooking using natural ingredients. Invite children to help. Use a cookbook such as *Nourishing Traditions,* by Sally Fallon.

Challenge: At Home

Read the labels on the foods you eat. For one day, challenge yourself to eat foods that have no more than five ingredients listed on the label. Do not buy cleaning supplies in which the ingredients are not listed. Put away antibacterial soaps. Carefully dispose of all other toxic cleaning supplies. Try switching to cloth napkins instead of paper. One day per week, eat meatless.

Sustainability in the Scriptures

Ho, everyone who thirsts,
*   come to the waters;*
and you that have no money,
*   come, buy and eat!*
Come, buy wine and milk
*   without money and without price.*
Why do you spend your money
*   for that which is not bread,*
and your labor for that which
*   does not satisfy?*
Listen carefully to me, and eat what is good,
*   and delight yourselves in rich food.*
Incline your ear, and come to me;
*   listen, so that you may live.*
*   Isaiah 55:1-3*

Did You Know?

Many name-brand household chemicals are harmful to our health, including some all-purpose cleaners, ammonia, antibacterial products and disinfectants, chlorine bleach, drain openers, furniture polish, metal cleaners, oven cleaners, rust removers, spot-and-stain removers, and toilet-bowl cleaners. To choose safer alternatives, look for products that do not contain the words c*aution, warning, danger,* or *poison.* The first two words indicate moderate hazards; the second two indicate high hazards. Scented products may also contribute to indoor air pollution and aggravate asthma and sensitive skin. Follow product instructions for the safest use. For more information on household cleaning products, go to *govlink.org/hazwaste/house/products.*

Better yet, make your own nontoxic cleaning supplies using ingredients such as baking soda, borax, distilled white vinegar, hydrogen peroxide, lemons, olive oil, vegetable-based liquid castile soap, and washing soda. For more information on making nontoxic cleaning supplies, go to *eartheasy.com/live_nontoxic_solutions.htm.*

We Did It!

Village Presbyterian Church in Prairie Village, Kansas, has greened its kitchen—no small feat for a 5,000-member church that prides itself on environmental stewardship. Dwight Tawney, administrative pastor, reports, "We serve 300 people every Wednesday night for dinner. Three years ago we were using paper, plastic, and Styrofoam. We disposed of 300 sets of that every single week. Now that's completely gone. We don't use it at all."

Gold and green melamine dishes grace the tables of their dining areas. Reusable silverware rounds out the table setting. The Styrofoam is long gone, as is the sizeable amount of trash generated each week. "There's a little tradeoff," Tawney notes. "We have to wash the dishes." Even so, the amount of water used to wash the dishes is insignificant compared with the manufacturing, transportation, and disposal process that used to be involved. Unlike smaller churches, a full kitchen staff takes care of cleanup here.

Not just the dishes have changed at Village Presbyterian; what is served on them has also changed. "In season we serve local produce," says Tawney. "And we have virtually eliminated fried food from our menu." A dietician attends the monthly meetings of the Environmental Action Committee. Not only does she bring great ideas to the table, she brings purchasing power.

Even so, purchasing decisions are carefully weighed for economic feasibility and environmental sustainability, which means the church uses paper napkins, albeit with a higher recycled content. After careful consideration, staff realized that the cost of laundering cloth napkins would be prohibitive.

Traditional cleaning supplies have been replaced with a greener alternative. "We now use low volatile organic compound (VOC) cleaning agents," Tawney says. "Our building superintendent is part of the Environmental Action Committee. It is important to have him in on the decision-making process." The superintendent helps them make and meet policy guidelines that keep this facility on the growing edge of green.

Even the coffee has gone green at Village Presbyterian. "We drink a lot of coffee here," Tawney says while giving a virtual tour of the facility. "We had coffee pots going all the time, but we were consuming a lot of energy and wasting a lot of product. Now we have on-demand coffee." Using a rental system that includes frozen coffee concentrate means no waste and a guaranteed fresh cup of coffee every time. "It actually ends up being cheaper," he says.

It is easy to reference intangibles such as carbon footprints when talking about the need for environmental stewardship, but all Tawney has to do is point to one steaming cup of coffee in a real mug. Through his eyes, it is easy to see that going green makes sense for the climate and the pocketbook.

10. Gifts of Administration: The Office

If worship is the church's heart, the office is its brain. Because of the office's daily activities, there are many opportunities to green it. Today's gifts of administration include knowing how to preserve the creation while running a church. Here we will take a look at mail, communications, paper, electricity, and electronics.

The Basics

- Cancel junk mail and unwanted catalogs. You will save time, energy, forests, and landfill space. The company will save money and natural resources.
- Trade out incandescent light bulbs for CFLs. Make use of electronic communications. Instead of creating your own paper junk mail, e-mail newsletters, stewardship reports, and other communications. Print a few copies for those who do not have e-mail or prefer not to use it.
- Turn off all electronics at the end of the day, including routers, printers, copiers, and computers.
- Unplug phone chargers when not in use.
- Program computers to go into sleep mode when you are away for 20 minutes or more. Screen savers are not the same as sleep mode.

- Save paper by reusing bulletins and bulletin inserts. If you hold more than one weekly worship service, adapt your bulletin to convey all the information necessary in one bulletin. Then collect bulletins at the end of each service and reuse throughout the morning or evening services. Consider printing fewer bulletins if you use screens and projectors in worship. There may be people who do not need them.
- Purchase reused printer cartridges, and refill or recycle the old ones.
- Use both sides of a piece of paper before you recycle.
- Recycle bulletins, paper, catalogs, newspapers, and other office refuse.
- Recycle electronics such as computers, copy machines, fax machines, and telephones.

Get Creative
- Get a Facebook page or other social networking page, and encourage members to connect that way. If you do not know how to set up a social networking page or site, ask tech-savvy members to help you.
- Use electronic invitations instead of paper to let people know about church functions. One site you might want to try is Evite (*evite.com*).

Go All Out

- Close the loop: Use recycled paper and office products, including copy paper, envelopes, folders, notebooks, pens, and trash liners. Wherever possible, look for 100 percent post-consumer-waste recyclable products.
- Institutionalize environmental stewardship by incorporating it into your mission and vision statements.

Challenge: At Home

Use both sides of paper before you recycle. Do not just toss your junk mail; cancel it. Purchase recycled paper and plastic products wherever possible. Reuse items wherever possible. Before making a new purchase, envision what will happen to it at the end of its useful life. If it will end up in the landfill, think twice before buying it. Then think again.

Sustainability in the Scriptures

For you shall go out in joy,
and be led back in peace;
the mountains and the hills before you
shall burst into song,
and all the trees of the fields shall clap their hands.

Psalm 55:12

Did You Know?

Junk mail is a huge waste of time and resources, and it depletes forests and clean water while adding to global warming. The average person receives 41 pounds of junk mail per year.[34]

Each year, the junk mail industry destroys about 100 million trees to produce its promos, pleas, and promises. The production and disposal of junk mail consumes more energy than three million cars. Each of us will spend an average of eight months of our lives dealing with junk mail.[35]

We Did It!

It is hard for Denise Ermentraut, the business manager at First Congregational Church in Longmont, Colorado, to remember what life was like before going green. "We've been doing it for so long here," she says. "It is just what we do."

For five years, this 373-member church situated at the foot of the Rocky Mountains has emphasized good financial and environmental stewardship. For the office staff of five, that means handling a lot less paper.

Thanks to a major enhancement of the church's website, its monthly newsletter, *The Courier*, is now available online, as are announcements, memos, and the Lenten devotional. The report for the May congregational meeting, the mainstay of a Congregational church, is uploaded to their site, too. Not everyone has e-mail, so a few copies of these documents are printed; but even that number has substantially decreased over time.

That is not to say the office is paperless. "The IRS wouldn't like it if I didn't have hard copies of some things," laughs Ermentraut. "But we've about cut our trash pickup in half. In fact, in March we cut back from two 96-gallon trash bins to one, reducing our monthly bill by $22."

The office is saving money and energy in other ways. Ermentraut reports, "We've programmed our computers and copier to power down when not in use. Every ten to fifteen minutes they go to sleep." In addition, a church-wide computer system regulates electricity usage and powers down equipment at night and at other times when it is not needed. The staff favors fresh air over air conditioning, and sunlight helps heat the office in winter.

In the office, First Congregational's emphasis on zero-waste takes many forms. The staff is quick to put a stop to junk mail and extra catalogues from suppliers. They are equally as quick to stop unwanted e-mail. You will not find drawers and shelves full of extra supplies there either. Instead, that space is taken up by gently used binders, file folders, and notebooks. "We just don't use as much as we used to," Ermentraut notes.

The dry climate makes using recycled paper in the copier a challenge, but Ermentraut and her staff have found other ways to be environmentally friendly. Printer cartridges get refilled. At mealtime, glass coffee cups, compostable paper plates, and flatware made from cornstarch are used instead of foam and plastic.

As you can see, First Congregational runs a lean operation. All of this means more money for ministry and fewer greenhouse gases emitted into the atmosphere.

At the same time that their carbon footprint has been shrinking, though, their spirit has been growing. Instead of a narrow focus on material things, they have expanded their focus on God's abundance, helping them see things in a whole new way. "We have big windows in the office," Ermentraut says. "With all this natural daylight, sometimes we don't even have to flip a switch."

How is that for seeing the light?

11. Go and Do Likewise: Missions

Salvation is meant for the whole creation. All too often we focus on one species alone: us. But who is watching out for those who cannot speak? Let your mission work include the forests, lakes, streams, mountains, grasslands, and all God's creatures that live there.

The Basics

- If you have not done so already, form a team to work on raising awareness within your congregation. See Step 1 in Part One of this book for more information.
- Whenever possible, encourage committees to use phone conferences instead of meeting in person. Meet before or after church to save extra travel.
- Ask your pastor to preach on the care of creation. Look for opportunities to incorporate this theme throughout the life of your church.
- Lead a small-group study using *Green Church: Reduce, Reuse, Recycle, Rejoice!*

Get Creative

- Think globally and act locally. Rethink missions. Not every mission trip has to include air travel and passports. Include local and regional projects on your mission agenda as well.

- Adopt a river, beachfront, wetland, forest, park, roadside, or other patch of land. Let this be your mission field. Plan a clean-up project. Restore a portion of creation to its natural beauty and functioning. Learn about the wildlife that frequents the area. Pray for it.
- Plant trees to offset carbon emissions from your mission-related travels.
- Conduct a churchwide campaign to help your congregational families go green. Read David Gershon's *Low Carbon Diet: A 30-Day Program to Lose 5,000 Pounds,* or go to *coolcongregations.com* for another approach.

Go All Out

- Find out what is going on in your church or denomination around the care of creation. Many church bodies are organized at the national level around this topic. Get involved.
- Sign up for environmentally oriented legislative alerts through your denomination.
- Join organizations such as Interfaith Power and Light, and learn from like-minded persons of many faiths.
- Contact your elected officials, and urge them to support responsible stewardship of natural resources.

- Write letters to the editor on matters pertaining to stewardship in your community.

Challenge: At Home

With your family, form a team to practice environmental stewardship at home. Participate in citizen democracy by pressing for the care of creation with your elected officials. Write letters to the editor. Offset your carbon emissions by planting trees.

Sustainability in the Scriptures

Go into all the world and proclaim
the good news to the whole creation.
                              Mark 16:15

Did You Know?

Think 350. According to the world's leading climate scientists, such as NASA's James Hansen, 350 parts per million (ppm) is the safe upper limit for carbon dioxide in our atmosphere.[36] At that number, the climate can be stabilized, avoiding catastrophic climate change. If we continue burning carbon-based fuels at the current rate, however, scientists estimate that we will be at 600 ppm of CO_2 by 2050.[37]

United Methodist author, educator, and environmentalist Bill McKibben has ignited a global grassroots movement to publicize this information. Religious groups were among the more than 5,200 actions that took place in 181 countries to call for a safe climate in preparation for global climate treaty talks held in Copenhagen, Denmark, in December 2009. To learn more, go to *350.org*.

We Did It!

At the start of its eighth decade, Church of the Crossroads (United Church of Christ) in Honolulu, Hawaii, continues to be at the forefront of social issues. One of the first interracial Congregational churches on the islands, Crossroads was formed when Hawaiian, Japanese, Chinese, Filipino, and Caucasian high school and college students decided to worship together.

In the early 1990's, the church became aware that the creation itself was at a crossroads. Pressing ecological issues prompted this proactive church to make stewardship of the earth one of its core tenets.

Since the church's ministry was founded on the principle of bringing diverse people together, it is no surprise that their environmental work also brings together the larger community. Crossroads, a church of about 200, recently became the nucleus of the Hawaii chapter of Interfaith Power and Light (IPL). Through this organization, Jewish, Buddhist, Hawaiian Cultural Spirituality, and Christian members—Protestant and Catholic —are taking a stand for a livable planet for future generations by addressing global warming.

The indefatigable Charles Pe'ape'amakawalu Burrows, known as Chuck or Doc, has been one of the guiding forces at Crossroads and Hawaii IPL. Part Hawaiian, he is a longtime church, community, and conservation leader.

"I grew up in the last days of the depression," he says. "Conservation and recycling were commonplace then." Raised on those values, he has since witnessed the effect that cheap fossil fuels have had on our society. "They power our current consumer-based economy and global warming, but we can no longer sustain that kind of economy. We have to help build a green economy, a sustainable economy, one that reflects new values. That's one of our key missions."

Church of the Crossroads has accepted that mission wholeheartedly. Led by a group of six advocates and with unwavering pastoral support, the church participated in the 2007 "Step it Up" campaign and the 2008 and 2009 "350" campaigns.

Hawaiians understand the importance of taking action. The islands are already experiencing an increase in the acidification of ocean waters due to an influx of CO_2. Warmer waters also mean more frequent hurricanes and bigger storm waves. "If ocean waters rise as predicted," says Burrows, "then Church of the Crossroads, which is three miles inland, will be at water's edge."

That sort of sobering reality prompts Burrows and his colleagues at the church to stay active. He says, "If a bill comes up that will reduce greenhouse gases, we're involved. We testify at the state and the national levels." Burrows believes in the power of faith to change individuals and families; but when it comes to the big picture, "it is going to take legislation."

Still, what drives Burrows is deeply personal. It is kinship. "When we look at life forms that exist on the earth and compare them to the concept of stewardship of creation," he says, "we realize that we have a family relationship. We have to care for our family wherever it may exist on earth."

12. The Gardener of Eden: Grounds

In Genesis 2, God is envisioned as a master gardener who designed, planted, and harvested the fertile garden of Eden. Out of this lush earth came every plant and creature known to humankind. Our purpose is to till it and keep it (Genesis 2:15). Today, we may not all be gardeners; but we can live out our high calling by practicing good stewardship of the land entrusted to us. Caring for the grounds of the church is a good place to start. In this section you will find ways to green your church grounds while supporting the dignity and integrity of creation.

The Basics

- Pick up trash, especially windblown plastic bags. These make a poor meal for birds and other forms of wildlife.
- Put out trash receptacles to encourage others to keep the grounds clean.
- Be bike-friendly. Set aside space in the parking lot for bike racks.
- Set lawnmower blades one notch higher. Longer grass means less evaporation, which means less watering.

- Mulch trees and plants. Chunks of bark, peat moss, or gravel keep the soil moist and discourage weed growth.

- Plant trees at the south and west to provide shade in summer. You can also plant trees as a wind block to cut down on winter heating bills.

- Plant appropriately for your climate. Choose native species instead of imported ones. In dry areas, xeriscape to conserve water.

- Plant perennials instead of annuals. These use less water, cost less money, and take less energy to keep up.

- Weed your gardens and lawns by hand; no need to use pesticides. After a good strong rain, or watering, the weeds come out easily.

- Discourage car idling in your parking lot. Newer vehicles only need 30-60 seconds to warm up. On average, two minutes of idling uses the same amount of energy it takes to drive one mile, all while getting zero miles per gallon.[38]

Get Creative

- Plant a community garden. Invite members and neighbors to grow their own gardens. Alternatively, give the produce away. Remember to leave the edges of the garden for "gleaning."

- Set aside another part of the lawn for a compost pile. This will enhance the soil without having to use petroleum-based fertilizers.

- Create a prayer garden. Make use of native trees, plants, and rocks to create an outdoor sanctuary for prayer, meditation, and reflection.
- Install a labyrinth—an ancient, compact walking path designed for reflection and renewal.

Go All Out

- Plant a sky garden if you have a flat, sturdy roof on your building. This type of green roof reduces storm-water runoff, increases green space, and beautifies the neighborhood, especially in urban settings. For more information, go to *greenroofs.com.*
- Plant a "Tree of Life" grove to offset carbon emissions, clean the air, hold soil and water in place, and foster biodiversity. Plant trees to commemorate baptisms, confirmations, weddings, ordinations, pilgrimages to the Holy Land, and other special occasions.
- Create a living churchyard by letting part of the lawn go wild. Mow just once a year. Create a safe space for birds, butterflies, insects, small animals, and a profusion of plants. Bless this sacred space. For more information, go to the site for Alliance of Religions and Conservation (*arcworld.org/projects.asp?project ID=271*) and Caring for God's Acre (*caringforgods acre.org.uk/*).

- Enlist local biologists or naturalists to conduct a survey of the plants and creatures that live around your church. Even in the city, nature abounds. Discover how to restore habitat that will nurture "the least of these."
- Protect and preserve special sites at your church by creating a nature center or nature trail on church grounds.

Challenge: At Home

Put the basics into practice at your home. Plant native trees in strategic locations. Not only do they sequester carbon dioxide, they will help with heating and cooling efforts. Remember to include the manse, rectory, or parsonage in your efforts.

Sustainability in the Scriptures

For the creation waits with eager longing for the revealing of the children of God; for the creation was subjected to futility, not of its own will but by the will of the one who subjected it, in hope that the creation itself will be set free from its bondage to decay and will obtain the freedom of the glory of the children of God.

Romans 8:19-21

Did You Know?

You can green your parking lot! Traditional asphalt parking lots prevent storm water runoff from filtering into the ground, which disrupts the local water cycle. Additionally, runoff dumps oil and petroleum byproducts into the water system. Using materials such as dirt, gravel, or grass pavers allows water to be reabsorbed into the ground. Incorporating tree islands reduce urban heat islands.

We Did It!

Chamblee United Methodist Church on the edge of Atlanta, Georgia, is a green oasis in an sprawling, land-locked city. Situated on 38 acres, this 1,000-member church has decided to keep its lovely green space open.

"We're trying to redefine progress here," explains the Reverend Jordan Thrasher, the 26-year-old associate pastor. "Instead of always building, we are striving to become excellent with what we have. Progress is about investing yourself in the place you are."

The church has done just that. Instead of expanding its buildings, the church has chosen to welcome neighbors to enjoy its woodlands, creek, 1.5-mile walking trail, and outdoor chapels. Under the leadership of Thrasher, who enjoys weaving together ecology and theology, this green space has drawn together a diverse community.

Church members and neighbors alike have invested in the land. Some clean the trails. Others look after the wildlife. One woman found and took an injured hawk to rehab. After the bird healed, she re-released it on the land. "The raptor lives here now," Thrasher said. "He's very happy. He'll perch on the steeple. I saw him the other day with something very big in his mouth." Another member of the church has a "chainsaw ministry." If he sees a tree that needs trimming or cutting down, he is right there. Others clean up the creek. "I saw old tires, even a kitchen sink in there, and lots of oil," says Thrasher. "We're going to make a start at restoration."

The green space has also opened doors to cross-cultural ministry. In one area, a garden is being cultivated by an elderly first-generation Korean couple. These members of the Korean Church of Atlanta share their produce with fellow church members.

Once overrun with kudzu, this restored green space has become a communal oasis. Now it is a natural place for children, young adults, families, and seniors—along with birds, animals, and trees—to enjoy and nurture one another.

Appendix: Building Green

Building from scratch is your chance to go green from the ground up. The greener the building, the better, because the biggest single source of emissions and energy consumption is architecture.[39] Almost half (48 percent) of the greenhouse gas emissions in the United States are due to the energy required to construct, heat, cool, and maintain buildings. Although the initial costs of building green are greater, as with any energy-efficient system, you will save money over the long haul while preserving the creation.

The Basics

Site

- Locate your building in the center of the community. Make it accessible to pedestrians, cyclists, and public transportation.
- Build up, not out. The smaller the physical footprint of the building, the easier it is to heat and cool, and the less open space it eats up.
- Protect and restore sensitive habitat.

Water Efficiency
- Make use of water-efficient landscaping.
- Use low-flow toilets.

Energy and Atmosphere

• Use highly efficient lighting systems.
• Use highly efficient heating and cooling systems.
• Use low-e windows.
• Incorporate green power.

Materials and Resources

• Choose materials with recycled content.
• Incorporate sustainably harvested woods.
• Use regionally produced materials.

Indoor Environmental Quality

• Choose low VOC paints, coatings, and floorings.
• Design for views.
• Allow natural daylight.
• Ensure access to fresh air, as well as heating and cooling controls.

Get Creative

• Install wind turbines or solar panels to produce electricity for the community.
• Plant edible landscapes that can feed the hungry.
• Choose locally produced materials and labor to support the local economy.
• Opt for low-e insulated glass for stained-glass windows.
• Reuse building materials by constructing around or upgrading an existing structure.

- Plant a living or green roof.
- Design a green parking lot.
- Install a grey-water system that reuses water for non-potable uses.

Go All Out

- Hire a LEED (Leadership in Energy and Environmental Design) certified architect. LEED is the industry standard for green building.
- Choose the level of LEED qualification you wish to achieve: Certified, Silver, Gold, or Platinum. While some congregations file for actual certification, others choose instead to direct these additional monies into mission and ministry.

Challenge: At Home

If you are building a new home, choose highly energy-efficient systems from the start. Look for the blue and white Energy Star on doors, windows, appliances, building materials, and heating and cooling systems. Incorporate LEED building and design principles wherever possible.

Sustainability in the Scriptures

Unless the LORD builds the house
*   those who build it labor in vain.*

*   Psalm 127:1*

Did You Know?

Buildings have embodied energy or "emergy." Precious resources such as water, fuel, wood, concrete, brick, glass, asphalt, metal—not to mention human effort and love—are all expended in the construction of a building. The manufacture, fabrication, delivery, and installation of materials have a carbon footprint, too.

Restoring or retrofitting an existing building with energy-efficient systems can be a great alternative to starting over. It conserves the "emergy" of your current building while saving new land from development.

We Did It!

The community food pantry, clothing closet, and computer ministry lab now have a new home in Prairie Village, Kansas. The old building that once housed this mission outpost has been replaced by a state-of-the-art green building. Deeply committed to good stewardship of resources, Village Presbyterian built smart from the start.

"We did a study first to see if we could reuse the building," explains Village Presbyterian's conscientious administrative pastor, Dwight Tawney. "But the old building was in miserable shape. A school built in the 1940's, it didn't meet any kind of code."

That is a common occurrence in this section of town. Five miles from their main campus, the mission outpost is located in the city core. From here, volunteers provide food, clothing, access to technology, training, and encouragement to the city's down-and-out.

While some people on the receiving end of good works are sometimes made to feel inferior, you would be hard pressed to feel that here. People's spirits are brightened just by walking through the doors.

A great seam of light runs the entire length of the building, brightening the main corridor from above with natural daylight. This skylight, made of clear insulated material, measures 175' long by 6' wide. No other lighting is needed during the day. When the sun sets, motion sensors turn on small T-5 fluorescent tubes as needed.

A solar array on the roof loops back into the electrical system and provides free cooling for the huge walk-in freezer stocked with food for the needy. Donated by someone who has a heart for the environment, it reveals the generous heart of this community of faith.

Heating comes from a ground-source heat pump. The savings are dramatic. "We're saving fifty percent on our heating bills," says Tawney, "even though we have more square footage and more building use during the week!"

Adding to the energy efficiency of the building are a computer-controlled thermostat that can be programmed and monitored from off campus, recycled building materials, nontoxic paint and flooring, and carpeting with a high recycled content. Low-maintenance land-scaping reduces the need for watering and mowing.

In some churches, you get the sense that it is all about the building. Not here. While Village Presbyterian worked with a LEED-certified architect and achieved a level between Silver and Gold, they kept the focus on missions. "In the end, because we're a non-profit, we didn't actually seek certification," Tawney says. "That would have cost an extra $40,000 and additional record-keeping. We thought it would be better to put that money into our main mission: caring for people."

Acknowledgments

Thanks to all the participants in my classes, presentations, and workshops who indicated the need for a book like this—you helped refine my ideas. Special thanks to David Gershon of the Empowerment Institute—your work continues to inspire me. I'm especially grateful to all the people who shared their stories with me—you have renewed my flagging faith and showed me what's possible. My deepest thanks remains, as always, reserved for my husband, Jerry Gonzales, whose love, sense of humor, and understanding make space for adventure.

Notes

[1] For more information about The National Religious Partnership for the Environment, go to *nrpe.org.*

[2] "Did You Know?" at *energystar.gov/index.cfm?c=small_business.sb_congregations.*

[3] "Compact Fluorescent Light Bulbs for Consumers," *energystar.gov/index.cfm?c=cfls.pr_cfls.*

[4] "2005 Warmest Year in Over a Century," *nasa.gov/vision/earth/environment/2005_warmest_prt.htm.*

[5] "Scientists Call for 80 Percent Drop in US Emissions by 2050 to Avoid Dangerous Warming," *Science Daily* (September 20, 2007).

[6] *Low Carbon Diet: A 30-day Program to Lose 5,000 Pounds,* by David Gershon (Empowerment Press, 2006); page 8.

[7] "Putting Energy Into Profits: ENERGY STAR® Guide for Small Business," *energystar.gov.*

[8] "The Future of Lighting: Scientists Create White Light That Is Eco-friendly, Affordable," by Sarah Bahari, *UNT Research,* Volume 18, Number 1 (Spring 2009), *unt.edu/untresearch/2008-2009/future-of-lighting.htm.*

[9] "Getting Started With LED Lighting," C. Crane Company, *ccrane.com/lights/led-light-bulbs/led-lighting.*

[10] "Change a Light, Change the World: 2007 Campaign Facts and Assumptions Sheet," *energystar.gov/ia/partners/promotions/change_light/downloads/CALFacts_and_Assumptions.pdf.*

[11] "Impact on Global Warming for Energy Saving CFL Lightbulb," Cut Your Footprint, *cutyourfootprint.com/lighting.asp.*

[12] "Our Vanishing Night," by Verlyn Linkenborg, *National Geographic* (November 2008).

[13] The first article of the Apostle's Creed is "I believe in God the creator of heaven and earth."

[14] "Energy Explained: Your Guide to Understanding Energy," US Energy Information Administration, *tonto.eia.doe.gov/energyexplained/?featureclicked=2&.*

[15] "Standby Power," Lawrence Berkeley National Laboratory, *standby.lbl.gov/*.

[16] "Fresh Ideas for Savings," Energy Star, *energystar.gov/ ia/partners/manuf_res/downloads/Refrigerator_ConsumerBrochure.pdf*.

[17] "Demand (Tankless or Instantaneous) Water Heaters," US Department of Energy, *energysavers.gov/your_home/water_heating/index. cfm/mytopic=12820*.

[18] "Small Wind Electric Systems," US Department of Energy, *energysavers.gov/your_home/electricity/index.cfm/mytopic=10880*.

[19] "Geothermal or Ground Source Heat Pumps," California Energy Commission Consumer Energy Center, *consumerenergycenter.org/home/heating_cooling/geothermal.html*.

[20] "When to Turn Off Personal Computers," US Department of Energy, *energysavers.gov/your_home/appliances/index.cfm/mytopic=10070*.

[21] "Heat and Cool Efficiently," Energy Star, *energystar.gov/index.cfm?c=heat_cool.pr_hvac*.

[22] "Heat Pump Systems," US Department of Energy, *energysavers.gov/your_home/space_heating_cooling/index.cfm/mytopic=12610*.

[23] National Council of Churches of Christ Eco-Justice Programs, *nccecojustice.org/water/water.php*.

[24] "Bottled Water Quality Investigation: 10 Major Brands, 38 Pollutants," by Olga Naidenko, Nneka Leiba, Renee Sharp, and Jane Houlihan, Environmental Working Group (October 15, 2008).

[25] Scripture taken from the Holy Bible, NEW INTERNATIONAL VERSION®. Copyright ©1973, 1978, 1984 by International Bible Society. All rights reserved throughout the world. Used by permission of International Bible Society.

[26] "Earth's Water Distribution," USGS: Water Science for Schools, *ga.water.usgs.gov/edu/waterdistribution.html* and "Top Water Conservation Tips," Planet Green, *planetgreen.discovery.com/go-green/green-water/green-water-top-tips.html*.

[27] "Why Worry About a Pound of Carbon Dioxide?" at Simple Steps, *simplesteps.org/home-garden/energy/why-worry-about-pound-carbon-dioxide*.

[28] "Large SUVs: What to Look For," ConsumerSearch, *consumersearch.com/large-suvs/important-features*.

[29]"Sipping Fuel and Saving Lives: Increasing Fuel Economy Without Sacrificing Safety," prepared for The International Council on Clean Transportation, by Deborah Gordon, David Greene, Marc Ross, and Tom Wenzel (June 2007), *theicct.org/documents/ICCT_SippingFuelFull_2007.pdf.*

[30]"Global Warming: What You Need to Know," The Pew Environment Group, *pewglobalwarming.org/resources/binder/basics_sources.html.*

[31]"EWG's Guide to Triclosan," Environmental Working Group, *ewg.org/node/26721.*

[32] "New Study: Common Air Fresheners Contain Chemicals That May Affect Human Reproductive Development," Natural Resources Defense Council (September 19, 2007), *nrdc.org/media/2007/070919.asp.*

[33]"Waste-to-Energy Reduces Greenhouse Gas Emissions," Energy Recovery Council, *energyrecoverycouncil.org/waste-energy-reduces-greenhouse-gas-emissions-a2966.*

[34]"Stop Junk Mail," *41pounds.org.*

[35]"Just the Facts: Junk Mail Facts and Figures," New American Dream, *newdream.org/junkmail/facts.php.*

[36] "350 Science," 350, *350.org/about/science.*

[37]"Climate Change," State of the World Forum: 2020 Climate Leadership Campaign, *worldforum.org/climate-change.htm.*

[38]"Should I Shut Off the Motor When I'm Idling My Car," California Energy Commission Consumer Energy Center, *consumerenergycenter.org/myths/idling.html.*

[39]"The Building Sector: A Hidden Culprit," Architecture 2030, *architecture2030.org/current_situation/building_sector.html.*